Made in the USA
Las Vegas, NV
01 March 2022

44806435R00081

DOES THIS DIVORCE MAKE ME LOOK FAT?

A Self-Help Guide to Getting Over it Already, Seriously Bitch.

NIKKI FRIAS

ISBN (paperback): 978-0-578-35374-6

Cover design by
Nikki Frias

Photography by
Kay Alayu Photography, LLC

Editing and Formatting by
Our Galaxy Publishing, LLC

ever seen myself as a writer. If someone would've
1e one day, I'd be a published author, I would've
1 my eyes in disbelief. I've been blessed with the
y to acknowledge the light within everyone else
1metimes struggle to see my own. I need to give
f the flowers I deserve. So, for the first time in a
, I'm selfishly dedicating this book to 2016 me.
We did it, bitch.

Table of Contents

A Word to the Reader

, thank you for paying my bills and taking the first
ecoming/regaining that boss-ass bitch you already
ou. If no one's told you today, you are strong.

 in a place of feeling broken, lost, or empty, I got
 dreaded holidays, birthdays, and past anniversaries.
d the loss of my old life and was fearful of the new
nsidered taking his ass back and being a stepmom,
 understand why everything happens for a reason. In
rds, you're not alone.

y has evolved, memories have faded, and honestly,
 to relive the difficult shit once you've healed. By
I mean I've learned to forgive. After enough therapy
ersations with myself, my divorce changed my life
etter. We both ended up getting what we wanted, a
 a career. Who knew it just wouldn't be together?

this book because it's what I needed five years
n I didn't know where to start. I struggled to find
 perspective on pain and how to cope with the
 of healing. So, I created it. My words have been
rewritten, and deleted again, but ultimately are from
f gratitude, understanding, and genuine honesty.

t get it twisted. We talk a little shit.

er the million-dollar question: *Does this divorce
 look fat?* No, I lost 200 pounds. It's a metaphor for
y ex-husband and the weight of my old life. We try
ittle deep here, and clearly, it needs an explanation.
u finish this book, I hope you'll see how far you've
 e excitement of knowing what is yet to come, and a

better understanding of who you've become.

And if you bought this book for weight loss, re-gift sister.

Please enjoy a life-changing piece of my story.

Oh, and don't worry, this book isn't long. I know never finish reading a damn book. Let me also en I'm "bitches."

Chapter One:
Ugh, Marriage.
Some Historical
Background.

vas definitely in my Top 8 on Myspace."

Tying the Maybe Not?

*Something old, something new, and she's some
else too.*

I never saw myself as the marrying type.

Growing up, I never dreamed about my wedding d
kids I would have. I rarely played house or with do
from my Baby Born (Circa 1991), because she p
foreshadowing of my 30's, I was more worried ab
regularity than societal norms.

From a family perspective, all major conv
surrounding how others should treat you (from bo
to what marriage truly meant) were non-existent.
divorce and navigating their own emotions, my par
too focused on surviving to break down how their
bitch daughter (me) should process. What can I
'90s were a crazy time with JNCO jeans and mul
butterfly hair clips. Keywords like "expectatic
"boundaries" were not used to express feelings. Ev
was surface level.

Even after their divorce, my childhood was a
but I can't remember when I had a conversation a
worth or what I deserved. I'm not trying to go th
my early emotional trauma, but I think you get tha
was a happy child, I have always struggled with e
relationships.

I met my husband when I was 18. Nelly and
Lunatics were the hottest rappers, and my days w
with wearing Baby Phat jeans and finding a holste
new Blackberry phone. I was in high school, and v
the Mexican restaurant while I was working. I noted

l red flag that he wore sleeping pants in public, but
 me get started. Our relationship progressed like
-year-old relationships; a lot of missionary sex,
 and no real problems. We would look forward to
 where we could spend our paycheck on each other
 many trips to the mall. Fast forward to graduating
we ended up moving in together and eventually got

 27, 2014, we wed amongst family and friends. On
ling day, my emotions were pretty apathetic. When
riting my vows, I had a friend ask me how I was
and my response was, "What's the worst that can
 We get a divorce?" And I meant it as if that wasn't
est red flag. My perception that the wedding and the
 itself was a page out of a Nicholas Sparks book
e. I didn't feel the warmth and fuzzies, we weren't
, and I wasn't in a space to recognize the signs.

been together for ten years in total, two-and-a-half
rried. On February 23, 2016, I filed for divorce.

t comes love, then comes marriage, then comes a
bad bitch?"

There were times universe was showing I was living the wrong and I ignored it. After m; signs, she'd had enou and said, 'Bitch, this going to hurt,' and gave an ultimatum to choo myself or someone else.

The Reason

Chapter Two:
ow Insert Ugly Cry.

*"And you don't even need cable
for this drama."*

Happy Wife? Better think twice

Oh, y'all got drama, drama.

I know, I know, get to the drama already. I figured
set up the scene before dropping some telenovela-ty

After about a year and a half of marriage, w
extremely comfortable but, quite frankly, not happy
relationship. I had gained 40 pounds and became emo
numb, knowing my husband was never home after
ever wanted to spend time with me. The signs poin
affair, but I was so confident in the person presente
I was unaware of his potential to devastate both of
completely.

It started when I found him parked near our house t
a woman on the phone, thanks, Bluetooth. Then bet
phone passcode constantly changing to the single en
I found while he was sleeping on our vacation in Ja
was clear that some shady shit was going down.

I mean, some women could tell me the writing wa
wall, but I guess that bitch was in braille.

As you've probably predicted already, he cheated
those rose-colored glasses like I was front row at
John concert, honey. The biggest issue, aside
happening, was the assumption I had that this perso
never, and could never, do this. I trusted blindly.
secure in my mediocre marriage that the possibili
crossed my mind.

How? When? Why? Where?

ere gut feelings, but I tried not to let my insecurities
y judgment. I'd always give the benefit of the doubt,
nights when he didn't come home, and his "Find
ids" oddly stopped working. But I have to say, that
Feeling was right. I wasn't crazy. The moments of
nd confusion were physical reactions to knowing
ispected was true; there was someone else.

also be stated that we tried therapy before the affair.
to feel the disconnect in our marriage and couldn't
s response that there was simply "something wrong
." So, I signed us up for couples counseling. We
it wasn't for us after the first few heated sessions
ematurely due to him wanting to wait in the car. I
one and pathetic by this point. I wondered if it was

ase enjoy the moment shit got real in story form.

anuary evening, the air was crisp when Nikki,
in workout clothes, entered the house after an old
mba class. "What is an old lady Zumba class?"
ht ask yourself. It's the 8 PM Zumba class where
imum age for participation is 60+, and features
om Miami royalty Mr. 305, Pitbull, and 2000's
n, Shakira.

husband sat on the love seat next to the overused
couch in the living room. The game was on, and
instantly was off. She walked over to greet her
and sat for a moment before getting into the
She looked at his face and knew something
ight.

?" she said in a concerned tone. He looked at her
ace that could only be explained after knowing a
for ten years. The type of look like someone died
did something they couldn't come back from.

15

He was somber with a calm demeanor, anticipa
storm that his half Dominican wife was about to
his ass; fucking Katrina style.

"I cheated."
Insert a fortissimo of stunned horns

She immediately knew. Between his face and t▍
review of how things in the last four months di▍
up, she knew.

"Why? When? Did you wear a condom?"

He hesitated, "Yes."

*Insert inner monologue: "I KNOW DAMN
THIS MOTHER FUCKER WHO REFUSES TO
A COAT IN THE COLD AND SUNSCREEN ▍
BEACH ISN'T GOING TO USE ANY FO▍
PROTECTION!"*

Instead of reacting and quickly planning his de▍
got up and took a shower.

The whole moment was an out-of-body exper
anticipated my inner Angela Bassett monolog▍
Waiting to Exhale would respond, and I'd storm
door as if the marriage never existed. Cue the infam▍
"That is trash!" after she burns all of her husband'▍
and car once finding out about his affair with a cow

The next couple of days were quiet. Once I was able
what happened, my logic moving forward was si▍
he wants to, he will. I'd known this man always to▍
and unmotivated, so I gave him the opportunity to▍
fight for this family. I told him that he would ha▍
everything to fix this marriage and, coming from a▍
who scheduled his dental appointments, did his laur▍

roceries, that was asking a lot. It was up to him. No
:uses as to why he could half-ass, like many things
ationship, but in the most Hollywood way possible.
his meant a better marriage and a sign that this was
wanted, or so I thought.

of weeks had passed, and my husband had regained
of the bed from his regular couch post. We weren't
:x, but we talked, which was a plus. I was exhausted
1g so angry that, a couple of days before, I decided I
onger going to be sad. I told myself that if I wanted
this marriage work, I had to do my part. I had to
to be successful, which meant making an effort to

particular morning, I got ready for work and hugged
and before leaving for the day. We hadn't hugged
le, but this morning it was different from his usual
ep 6 AM side hug. This hug had an intention,
onger than usual, tight (that's what she said,) and
ful. I told myself, "Everything is going to be okay.
oing to be okay."

he rest of my day looking for things that made me
om coffee to funny banter with coworkers. I even
ooking up cheap lingerie on Amazon to add some
our future hot and steamy new sex life. The day was
quickly, and I texted him to see if he wanted to see a
Yeah!" he responded. I wanted to start getting back
hings that made us happy--that was my contribution.

me, walked the dog, and waited for him to come

ever came.

ease enjoy the moment shit got real **real** in story

17

Daylight savings was not on her side, as Nikki r
was getting darker, and she hadn't heard from her
It had been a while since the couple planned a da
which was a positive sign for their recent rocky r
Nikki reviewed his last response, saying he should
soon, sent at 5:56 PM. It was now 6:30, and he was
answering her phone calls. The lack of response ga
uncomfortable feeling in the pit of her stomach.

She texted him: Hey, where are you? (Autor
assuming he's somewhere he shouldn't be.)
Him: Hey, have you been downstairs?
Her: No.
Him: Well, I left you something in the bedroom.
Her: Okay.

Walking to their room, she assumed a surpr
anticipatory room full of roses, and a dress on the
a letter saying, "Get dressed! I have an evening p
But instead, she was greeted with a six-page let
words like, "You deserve so much better" and, "I

She called him, and he immediately picked
conversation had long pauses that added to the dr
She could tell he'd been crying.

"What is going on?" she asked, trying to contain h

"She's pregnant and not going to get an abortion;
up." He was a wreck. She recanted the times th
trying to have a baby of their own and how he p
start trying while he knew he had one on the way.

Can a bitch enjoy her coffee and figure out her caree
dealing with her husband being a baby daddy?

Unfortunately, after 20 minutes, the time limi
Compassionate Nikki. **She was now in** *Call a Gro*

while Reminding Him You are That Bitch while ff Your TJ Maxx Gold-Plated Hoops and Applying taphorical Vaseline to that Ass mode. **After her ute verbal boxing match, he got quiet, and the it.**

ere are you?
eft.

a fortissimo of stunned horns again*

g ding ding, DOWN GOES FRAZIER!

)wn for seven days to stay with his family ten hours figured he couldn't deal with the pressure of his ns. By the time we got off the phone, he'd already ree states, and there was no chance of him turning

d on the phone that night and continued throughout . We hadn't talked that much since we first started)ur conversations included a level of adolescence ie playfulness and joking. I think it was our way of ince this was the first time in our lives together that to deal with highly mature issues and the splitting . He thought there was a chance too, but our new nent eventually transitioned to survival mode.

know when he was coming back, and after laying)uch for three days, I decided to tackle my original : "What the fuck are you going to do?"

should never be on speed dial, especially when iarried."

Once you heal from something, you'll never b the same. You'll be bette

The Response

Chapter Three:
Damn, Bitch.
What now?

we just go back to when it was easy?"

A Quick Reminder
to Respect the Basics.

You + Body Needs= Basics.

The grieving process looks different for everyone
me, it was gross.

I cried a lot. Picture watching *Marley and Me* whi
the spiciest chili and listening to John Lennon's
Christmas" on repeat. That kind of crying. My face
were sore from the breakdowns, and I was incons
learned the physical pain of sadness.

I didn't eat, speak, shower, or move for the first
barely felt alive.

Once I started telling friends and family, I got the
line of questioning. I was fortunate enough to
privilege to get those reminders, but just in case you

Did you eat, drink, and move your body today?

Respecting the basics is simple: stay alive and
your body. We can be devastated, but we can't be
malnourished over a man.

Fuck that.

Just Start Anywhere.

ust keep swimming. Just keep swimming."

/as a child, I've never done well with change. Some
gue it's a way to control situations, but others might
t's because I'm a Capricorn. Luckily, with a lot of
and personal growth, I admit it's wholeheartedly
ntrol. I struggle with letting go of the reins and
hings be. As you'd assume, the surprise of my
ed divorce was not one of those things.

ing care of the basics, my mind immediately went
ering the divorce, understanding my feelings, and
ng how I would move forward in the three days I
from work. I felt like I needed to regain control over
which meant planning and finding any way possible
ck to normalcy.

d the concept of taking time to grasp what was
ig, immediately started researching divorce lawyers,
ted a spreadsheet of assets. I figured if I were busy,
't need to process. Until my emotions hit me with a
down, bitch," and I started to squander. This mindset
alistic and not ideal, but this new life-altering change
uncomfortable. My reactive responses of "make it
rned into mush. By this point, I was no longer in
f I didn't slow down and allow things to process
, I wasn't going to recover. I had to get out of my
I took a back seat and started to do what I could.

ned. A form of meditation, cleaning allows you to
on one thing–scrubbing. I'm not sure if it was the
t high from all the bleach but throwing away the
rom my three-day couch sabbatical took my mind

off my feelings. Find other things that come easy
and require minimal efforts, like knitting or pain

• **Binged a new show.** The good thing about
numbing TV is you get invested in someone else'
and it takes you away from your reality. In 30 n
you can laugh and happily cry. I started *The Off*
coworker used to say I was the Kelly of the office
is entirely true,) and I'd always heard it was funr
watched it back-to-back four times now.

• **Packed.** Figure out where you're going an
accordingly. If you're able to leave, pack your life a
purging your things. There is something therapeuti
physically separating items you shared. Those ca
movie tickets no longer hold value. I left everythin
the ring, our wedding photos to a box with ten y
memories, movie tickets, and holiday cards. A joke to
it was a privilege to go home and sleep in my childho

The positive result of starting anywhere is the
you've started. Bravo! It's like taking it one day at a
through simple actions. Tackling the smaller items
To-Do life list only makes room for the more sig
"Yes, bitch. You did that!" possible. So, get up. No

"When life gives you trash, at least take a show

o One Cares (it's a good thing).

sorry to hear, but does that mean you can't make the happy hour?

person at work who overshares, never really focuses
ctual job, and talks everyone into ordering take-
he third time that week. So, after my brief hiatus,
m texted, "Where you at?" and I had to go back
I was super anxious, anticipating a suspicious line
oning. I mean, the loud, funny coworker is out for
s randomly without a planned vacation or sickness.
ppened?

ed when I came back, someone would notice
en eyes, fake smile, and lack of interest in my
ce. I thought they'd see my energy was low, and
the bathroom multiple times throughout the day. I
the conversations about my weekend, asking what
nd what we had planned for Valentine's Day. Did
n this all happened around Valentine's Day? Fuck.
I was not ready to go back.

Monday, and it had been five days since learning
e baby. I got up that morning and made the best
look presentable for the day. My mirror pep talk
d of, "You got this," and "Don't let them see you
tch." I drove to work, listened to a podcast, and
my morning coffee. I was one of the first people in
ed on my computer like any other day. Nothing had
, everything exactly where it was before I left, even
plant in the corner. I sat waiting for my computer to
nd saw a coworker walking towards me.

k, damn not Todd. Not IT, Todd! He was infamous

for asking intrusive questions, farting, and chewing
mouth open—a true man of mystery.

I tensed up, unsure of what he would say, and then s
magical happened. He said, "Good morning," and
right past me. That was it. Nothing happened. The re
day proceeded smoothly, and eventually; I went h
one asked any questions or pried for information be
one knew or even noticed.

So, after that moment, I realized two things:

- **No one cares (in a good way).** What do y
when you think about anything good, bad, excit
devastating that happens to someone you know
send a text, congratulate them with balloons, sen
flowers for grieving, bring them food, etc., but tl
harsh as it sounds) you go back to dealing with yo
goals and obstacles. It's normal, not insensitive, a
all do it.

I noticed this when I would tell my close friends and
about what happened. They'd cried with me, cl
in, offered to help move, but at the end of the da
still had their shit to handle. Take no offense. It's l
The practical side of this logic, especially in the
is that you have time to process without distractic
eventually, people forget. You won't always be the t
conversation, and over time, the scarlet letter "D" wi

- **You control the narrative of your story.** Since
cares, everything about your situation is on your ow
with whatever you want to tell or don't tell. You don
anyone a damn thing, so treat your story and op
when sharing the same way. Remember, the audien
knows the narrative from your perception, and you
story. Never succumb to the pressure of feeling li
have to tell everyone everything. People are always

an opinion, and given the situation, sometimes
ou have to say doesn't matter, either way, so say
true to you.

do care, but the quicker you look at your behavioral
s, you can adopt a better mindset towards healing.
ill not be the only time you'll be sad, but you won't
 forever. Remember how you cope when others
and know that's all around you.

that sucks. Will you still be able to make it to happy
Hunker down at work and only answer the hard
s when you know the answers.

"Life and people are constantly evolving."

Divorce like A Boss

What's in a word?

Have you ever noticed the response after you tell you're divorced? They react like it's a death. I'v found the word to be so intimidating. For the first years, I dreaded answering when people asked abou stopped. Instead of just giving myself the dreaded "I people the truth.

"It was the best thing to ever happen to me."

I meant it.

I made "divorce" a homonym—the same word different meanings.

Divorce: sadness, heartbreak, depression, loss, n drama, upset, anger, trauma.

or

Divorce: restart, growth, healing, independenc changing, and at some point, happiness.

Weigh your options. You made an effort to try and marriage, and guess what? It didn't work out, a okay. Stop telling yourself that divorcing makes yo of person who is "unlovable" or "difficult." Reclai empower it! Divorce is whatever you want it to be, others expect. So, change the narrative with an emp who you are now.

u meet with the lawyers, assets are split, and the
e signed, you have to decide what moves forward.
een killing every other aspect of your life, don't let
ore than a pothole on the highway of your dreams.

"First you empower, then you conquer."

You Will Consider Going Bac

People make mistakes, right?

I always said I wasn't going back, but I tried e
knowing about the affair and the baby. I could h
disrespect is the closure" after I'd succumb to re
to a good morning text or would find myself gettin
about random "I'm sorry" flowers from my husban

We went on a couple of dates, and I'd sit at a tab
from my husband, hoping this would feel normal
He'd say comments like, "I can't wait until we have
kids," as if our shared appetizer meant we could
to Taco Tuesday and joint-friend Christmas partie
officially a sign he had lost his fucking mind, but a
to hear.

My way of coping was forgetting and believing n
was real. I'd pray she was lying, and I made a lot of
for his behavior. I'd write in my journal, "Maybe
actually save us," and, "I think we are getting stro
if there was a chance, we were able to survive th
what a fucking lie.

On one of our last dates, he said, "I wish you were p
too. So, we could be together," and that's when re
He wanted to forget as well, even at the cost of my
After that night, I told myself no more dates and
allowing him to have his cake and baby mama
hard part about divorce was how tempting it was
We show our strength in different ways, but I
like I didn't want him to do everything I needed
the man I wanted him to be. So, I considered my

e have shared assets? *No.*

want to sacrifice myself for a non-biological child?
no.

on his best day, was this worth it? *Fuck, no.*

fear of being alone more than being in a blended
? *No.* I'm the Sofia Vergara of my life, but this
o *Modern Family.*

reason why I thought of staying was the negative
f being a divorced woman, single in her late
without children. I could hear the fuck boys of
e screaming, "She must be infertile or crazy," as
right. So, I considered these options as well.

still have children? *Fuck, yes.*

re an age limit on marriage? *Uh, no.*

want to have kids? *Eh, maybe?*

go over my marriage quota? *Well, yeah.* I only
d it to be once, but this was considered a practice.
.

my questions emphasized children and marrying
ture, but make sure your list aligns with what
t for your life. When considering your options,
out the things you value and if it would be
with another person or situation. For example:

ou financially independent?

ou trust them again?

his affect your quality of life?

u weigh the longevity vs. the quality?

ou able to move past this?

you see yourself just as happy, or happier, with a
erson?

ill be quick to judge a woman for considering the
f staying in a relationship after infidelity, and, aside
eing no one's fucking business, you need to figure

out what best makes sense for you. Sometimes the
to stay is a lot deeper than societal expectations. Yo
might've been your best friend, soul mate, or lif
and while it's devastating, deciding to stay is stil
option.

You're not a robot, and your life is not a movie.
closure or rethinking your option of leaving is oka

Whatever decision you make for the life you want, r
to give yourself grace and fuck everything else.

"Should I stay, or should I go now?"

3ite the Bullet. Go to Therapy.

Get a Nancy.

was very foreign to me before my divorce. The
ication of feelings and thoughts within my marriage
l of questions like, "You good?" or, "Do you need
utes?" We met at 18, and ten years later, we still
icated like we were kids. I decided to give therapy
er talking with loving friends and family wasn't
Yeah, I had my tribe, but a part of me still needed
struct how I let this happen to me, why it occurred
nd who the fuck I was after this. My mission was to
y some of the emotional baggage that was weighing
n (that bitch was like a high school backpack), and
to use that good insurance before leaving his ass.

was my first-time doing therapy alone, I felt a little
lmed about where to start. I did a google search
ed to a couple of different receptionists who left
s for me or immediately told me the pricing. A lot
of my budget, like $200 a session, and they didn't
insurance, but I kept looking.

e new to therapy, remember you don't have to
consider yourself Goldilocks when it comes to
Some might be too hot and some too cold. Find
that's just right. If you're not able to connect after
of sessions, move on. Therapy requires a lot of
ility and honesty, and you need to make sure you
environment that harbors those sentiments.

e of days later, I got a call back from one of my
ice messages. Her name was Nancy, and she was
e of wit, spice, and honesty that I needed. After

one conversation with Nancy, I knew she was
She sounded older and impatient to hear the bull
immediately wanted the reasoning behind my v
conversation was pretty short:

Nancy: Hello, Nikki. What's your reason for
therapy?
Me: Hey, Nancy. My husband had an affair, and
woman is pregnant.
Nancy: Oh, shit.
Me: Yeah.

The chance of finding a good therapist that
personality mixed with a ridiculous level of cursing
took my insurance seemed impossible. But just li
booked my appointment for the next week.

Meeting Nancy wasn't what I was expecting. Sh
her 70's, with white hair and a frail body. Her o
outdated, with little trinkets to show her personality
across from me at a desk, contrary to the chair ne
lay-down couch. No, I did not lay down, and no, s
sit next to me, humming and sighing from every r
We started our first session catching up like gi
Surprisingly, we didn't talk much about my ex
upbringing and family dynamics. I was surprised t
was not on my immediate problems but my identity.
conversation felt like a minute, and I left with que
cried a lot, as expected, but interestingly, it wasn'
reasons I thought. I was crying about my self-w
fears. As it turns out, I was so focused on fixing my
and marriage; I suppressed my efforts to fix myself.

During our months together, I learned the pre
balancing the stress of my marriage, my emotiona
from childhood, and learning more about who
started to notice how little Nancy and I had to ta
over the three months of my visiting. Eventually,

34

austed about the topic, and it showed. I initially
e a week, then two weeks, then monthly.

erse had a funny way of showing me my progress,
certain point, I no longer needed to see Nancy. Let
by saying I love the elderly, but I caught Nancy
on the job in the middle of me talking a couple
. Now, I know I can talk, but in the middle of a
? During one of our conversations, she asked a
and, while I was answering, I could see her eyes
heavier

falling asleep?" I asked, and her eyes immediately

defensive. "I am not." I felt like a parent was
ding me.

alking and then sat in silence because she fell
hile writing notes! We sat for about five minutes
ted for her cat nap to finish. It was one of the
vkward situations I've ever been. My copay
therapy, not a sleep study. After that, I knew
were tired of hearing about the same shit.

of advice: If your therapist falls asleep during a
you've talked a little too much, or her sugar is low.

side, find your Nancy, tell her all your feelings, and
hit out. Therapy is essential for your progress. It can
nfortable and awkward, but it helps paint a picture
ou process, react, and proceed. Drop the ego and get
learn more about your damn self. Trauma doesn't
ok or specific response. It's a forced change in you.
ile you can't change what has already happened,
rself the best opportunity to learn from it.

is meant to help you, so take advantage of it when

you can. Who knew your childhood, self-percept
other relationships molded you into the person
today? I did not. News Flash! No one is "normal
you think you don't need therapy, you do!

"Talking about the same thing over and over aga.
eventually force you to find a solution."

Accept You Might Fuck Up Along The Way (literally).

Mom and dad, please skip this chapter.

edly played wife after we separated. We'd go on
dates and talk about future plans like when we
ted dating. One night after drinking, we had sex.
igly, it was some of the best sex we'd ever had, but
d've been the three dirty martinis talking.

inutes later, after it was over (*muhahaha fuck y'all,
book!*), we laid in bed, and I burst into tears. I felt
and immediately regretted what had happened. I
ome form of familiarity, and I let my emotions get
of me. I wanted to be close to him again and not feel
alone anymore. I felt like shit, while I think he took
nall glimmer of hope for us. For the next couple of
he rubbed my back as I sobbed. This was my post-sex
wn, and it felt icky. I needed a shower to rid myself of
e and, well, vodka.

xt morning, I woke up alone, hungover, and
sed, the worst combination ever. I knew I couldn't
ne, so I waited until therapy that day to process. I
icy all the goods.

ough I anticipated a long conversation about not
ck and learning my lesson, she seemed unfazed. She
on't be so hard on yourself," and shrugged it off like
thing in the most unenthused tone. Nancy seemed
ed. My guilt was overwhelming.

e I'd betrayed myself and everyone rallying around

me. The long conversations about how I deserved b
daily check-ins seemed like a waste of time after ter
returning to my husband. I kept my head low for th
the day and tried to hold my secret for as long as
until I told my best friend.

"We had sex," I said, and similar to Nancy's respe
too seemed like it wasn't a big deal. "Nik, you are n
him, and well, shit happens." I had two people in n
telling me to let it go, so I tried my best not to fee
Once I was able to show my face in public again,
turned into a purging.

Unlike that one girlfriend we all have who kee
back to that one shithead boyfriend, the drunken
cleansing for me. I had very conflicting feelings fe
time, so the physical response I had after sex sho
what I expected was a farse. The actual act was ve
and full of emotion, but as we all know, the physi
sex is a small percentage of a person. We've seen
one-nightstands and, well, fucking your soon-t
husband. Sex was the easy part, and once I realized
lost, it was a little easier accepting our fate. I lea
hard way (literally) fucking up was inevitable and
the process.

Whether you allow disrespect, have unexpected s
him back when you know he's lying, or turn the
something you know that's wrong it's all beneficial

• **A physical reaction can mean a lot.** That gut
when something isn't right or the wave of anxiety
you're around certain people says a lot. Listen
body. It's saying everything you don't want to. Aft
I felt bad, physically weak.

• **Experience provides perspective.** Show up
him the benefit of the doubt, and let whatever ha

, I know it sounds like a reach, but giving him
ortunity and truly being opened to saving your
e leaves you with no question of, "What if?"
ve signed those papers, I knew there was not much
ould've done.

times, indulging is necessary. Like that piece of
te during a diet, sometimes we have to indulge in
ires to know what we want. My mind made our sex
tful and romantic, which realistically was not true.
d to only think of the good times, and indulging
ninder that it's not all hype you conjured up from
y.

rds of a woman on the other side, shit does happen,
ompletely normal. We all have moments we regret
oubling times. Sometimes, it seems necessary. Just
a moment of weakness convince you you're a weak
u're not; just horny and sad.

that a way to cope with sadness, or are you just
happy to see me?"

New Person. Who Dis?

You aren't going to be the same. You'll be be

I had a coworker say to me, "You've always had a s
always will, but this will change you." I didn't kr
to take it, but it hit me like a bag of bricks. I didn'
be different. I knew who I was and, while this div
a setback, I anticipated I'd eventually be the same
prided myself on being strong and unaffected by a
This would not break me.

Fast forward. The change happened, but not like I e

It wasn't the cliche, "I am stronger," or, "I am more
press tour I had anticipated. I was hardened and n
expectations and hopes I had of people faded, and th
love amplified. I lost hope in people or a future with
The tortilla chip on my shoulder grew, and I becan
I hated how a situation out of my control affected n

I didn't want to be different. I wanted to be myself, u
and original. I know it's not realistic, but once I acce
change, I had to relearn who I was. *If I'm not me, t
is she?* I worried these scorned feelings would be
identity.

There will be a moment when someone will shine a
how hard or impatient or insensitive you are, and the
see shit is different. You'll go into situations expect
worst in people, and when things go bad, you do
wince. That is the moment you need to actively
piece from the chip on your shoulder and not let th
situations change your morality. The biggest obst

hat loss and making myself better. Guarded but onically, my divorce led me to my truest self.

ker you're able to accept that life experiences change quicker you can learn that the characteristics you've ke you better. Experience alone requires change, it's erpower, but strategically you have to maintain a between cautious and callous. The initial acceptance different is hard because we don't know what it out its redirection only promotes opportunities for ment. Turn that hurt into a reminder that you aren't on anymore, and for a good reason.

ght has only strengthened. You'll learn being isn't a bad thing. It's a result of growth. How can and not be better? You are different. You've grown ations, traumas and now can turn your response ver. To overcome depression, sadness, strife, and e, you've built a resume of resilience and recovery. ce forces your light to amplify, never dim. You are , dammit!

A note to my future husband, this bitch is lit."

Never Forget the Feeling.

Because you will forget.

I made a doctor's appointment after it was know
having unprotected sex with another person. The
we met, I was talking about ovulation and our
expand our family, and now I was asking for an ST

Curious, my doctor asked, "The last time you w
we talked about trying for a baby. What happene
didn't expect that I'd be in this place months after
conversation.

They took my blood, and I had to wait a couple of day
the results. In that time, my toxic ass looked up celeb
Magic Johnson and Charlie Sheen, anticipating th
Yes, that is a toxic trait, and no, I would not rec
googling HIV information while waiting for yo
results.

For the first time in my life, I had no say over my
trusted someone, and they made decisions that pl
affected me, which was horrifying. I called my girlf
next day about my negative test results and, after ce
another small victory, she said, "Remember this fe
didn't realize the impact of those words at the mome
was something I used as a tool in my healing journe

We all remember the name of our first kiss or bully,
moment in time that exudes an emotional reaction yo

get. Once you've decided that the relationship is not
forward, start taking mental snapshots of moments
anxiety, stress, sadness, and trauma. It could've
nething he said or something you had to do from
as, like an STD test. Those moments you felt small
rd, keep them at the forefront of your mind, along
n you lost your virginity and the first time you tried
not, the memories will fade.

a funny way of allowing us to forget how things
feel. It makes forgiveness a lot easier, but once
as, you're left with your formed memory of what
d. In hindsight, those instances were less miserable,
bad than the actual experience. It's like your mind
cess past the current moment of feelings. I couldn't
now I felt yesterday, better yet, last year. So, having
moments that took you to that emotional state allows
nderstand why all the work of divorce is necessary.

se mental notes, honey! It will help you understand
won't deal with his ass again. Time does heal all
but remembering specific feelings reminds us why
the first place and why we won't go back.

"It wasn't even that bad? Yes, bitch, it was!

Have Y'all Met Patty?

Petty Patty is here to partay!

Let's face it, being the bigger person is hard at requires maturity and emotional awareness. Who's for that shit? Allow me to introduce you to Petty Pai the voice in the back of your mind that talks you ir all the wrong things to make you feel better. The tru feeling is temporary. For the moments we want to b valuables, roll into his job to make a scene, find her, and even change the Wi-Fi password, Petty P. all of us. She has four phases:

1. She wonders.
2. She gives a false reality of the wonder.
3. She reacts to the false wonder.
4. She feels like shit.

I prided myself on taking the higher road throug situation, but when I didn't hear from him one n mind immediately went into destructive mode. getting a divorce, but I still felt like I had the aut check on him and express my disdain for his transg

I was driving home from work late that night, and h answering his phone. I could hear Patty saying:

Is he with her?
What is he doing?
Why isn't he answering?
I got closer to the exit of the home we shared and

a pit stop. My anxiety was at an all-time high,
ing what I was about to confront. It was a physical
of, "It's not worth it! This is not worth it!" But I
ing and pulled up to an empty home with two empty
pots.

f saying, "You were wrong," and heading to my
atty started yelling, "He's with her!" and presented
of him lying in bed with a faceless woman, laughing
g happy and it ate me up. I immediately called him
back until he answered.

seventh call, he finally answered, and I popped
accusations and questions of what he was doing. I
and finally showed my cards. I was generally non-
ational, but my emotions got the best of me, and my
ngs turned into anger.

with that *bitch*? What the fuck are you doing?" His
was confusion, not expecting me out of character
om Friday night. It turned out he was at the casino.
ear a poker table set up and older men talking in the
nd.

got off the phone, I felt stupid. I let Patty work her
my thoughts and immediately regretted my reaction
thetical scenario. I've never been the fighting type.
as ready to rumble over a man I didn't want. The
t after the whole situation made me rethink how I
rvive this divorce, and that was getting rid of Patty.
to go. She wasn't any good for me. Every time I let
me down a path of delusion, I ended up on my face
dded wound to heal. It became exhausting.

nd ways to pivot.

de Actual Logic. Was Petty coming from a place
h? Did this really happen? Where did this logic

come from? My feelings or actuality? Confron
Patty is saying with logic, since what she put in you
didn't come from a place of understanding. Rem
she wants all the drama.

• **Good Distraction.** Not social media, but a
dinner with friends, hiking, make it a point to get
that mindset. Change your environment and wate
much better you'll feel.

• **Flip it and Reverse it.** We tend to go toward the n
in times when we feel like shit. Try flipping the o
of what Patty is saying. Think of the outcome of
positively.

In that instance, instead of driving past his house, I s
said, "He's probably playing a video game or poke
that was what he usually did. People don't change
their routines, so the likelihood of what I expected
Combat those negative thoughts head-on!

• **Think of the Outcomes.** I didn't know what
getting into when I decided to go to his home, but
it would hurt. Even not seeing his car in the parkin
was an instant punch to the stomach. Who's to sa
would've happened if what I anticipated was re
fight, I curse her and him out, the police are called, o
are made, I go to jail, the possibilities are endless
sure you take a beat to assess the situation and rev
the outcomes. It's never worth it, especially if you
in prison. These mother-bearing hips in a jumpsui
bye.

Chuck the deuces to Petty Patty. She was never your

Now, Figure it Out.

u have no choice, and also all the choices.

divorce, there was something to revel in, knowing
decisions no longer affected another person, and
timidating. After we signed the papers, I had the
ision of figuring out what I wanted my new life to
. I knew the adjectives I wanted, but the nouns were
iefine. So, I started with my job. It was a primary
 my unhappiness, and I desperately wanted to make
.

ted with everything I hated.

's a superpower to know what I want most of the
m men to food, I can tell you with one conversation,
if it's something I want—both are interchangeable.

 so meticulous about many things in life, but I
l with answering, "What did I want?" The answer
o simple since it was from me, but it wasn't. I could
he specificity of why I hate the smell of lavender
ds like "pungent" or "putrid," but when it came to
anted to do with my life, I only could respond with,
y," and Kanye shrug an "I don't know."

itred as an asset. I took all the things I didn't want
 job, relationship, goal, etc., and started the process
iation. For example, during the six years I had a
 job, I struggled with the idea of living for the
 after working 40 hours. You wake up at 7 AM,
eight, and punch in at nine. You dread Mondays and
sional birthday cake soiree with the close talkers
ounting. That Costco sheet cake and lifestyle isn't

good enough, and you know it! So, start somewher

• **Write down your non-negotiables.** Non-nego
are the things that drain your soul. It can be eme
mental, or physical. Whatever emits a feeling yo
enjoy. Then, isolate what particular issue that cha
you. For me, it was my career. I struggled with
purpose in the jobs I'd accepted in the past and f
I was wasting time. I knew it was required, but I
longer willing to accept a job that didn't feed my s

• **Find what feeds you and your soul.** Create pr
cons lists for your next ideal job. Find a mixture
pose and enjoyment for you to survive. Answer th
tion, "What makes you want to get up every mor
and answer that with purpose. Be a little flexib
some of your cons since nothing is ever perfect, b
firm with your pros. Go in with the mindset of
what you want, no exceptions.

> PROs: Helping people
> Flexible schedule
> Feeling utilized
> Collaborative environment
>
> CONS: Low Salary
> Micromanager
> No work/ life balance

It's the process of elimination, folks. Instead of
recreate the wheel with new ideas that will make
the life you've always wanted, start by eliminating t
that don't bring joy, give you anxiety, stress you
out, or cost too much money. Enough is enough.

• **Be open to the idea of what you want, le
different.** If you're writing down what you wa
won't settle for anything less, be open to the idea

differently. Fulfillment can come in multiple
and it's about what fulfills you at the end of the
rew the expectation of what you think people want
. Make that shit work for yourself.'

a park ranger or Power Ranger, don't just accept
if it's not what makes you happy.

*s too short to minimize your screen whenever your
boss walks by."*

Chapter Four:
h, It's Like That?"

"Divorce is the easy part.
Healing requires work."

Get a Fucking Anthem.

*"You Don't Have to Call" by Usher
and "Just Fine" by Mary J Blige.*

Like the intros for baseball players at the game
music before a night out, we all have those songs t
us feel good. Something that builds you up and rem
of who you were before shit went left. It's a pick-m
has nothing to do with his broke ass.

Music provides comfort. It helps us express our
and has the power to validate our emotions. Whe
through hardships, we assume we're alone, and no
understand until we hear the Lemonade album an
it, unfortunately, happens to everyone. Beyonce go
on. I got cheated on. I am, in fact, Beyonce.

On the nights I didn't want to talk but wanted to ge
take the good ol' Ford Hatchback out for a ride to
anthems. After a couple of drives, I felt so clear-mi
it quickly became a part of my weekly schedule.

Tips for knowing it's an anthem song:

- You yell, "Oh, shit!" and turn it up as loud as pos
  when it starts.
- You clear your throat during the interlude to mak
  for the screaming, or well, singing.
- It incites any form of gyration.

I had so many anthems. They would be played acc
what I was doing. Usher and Mary J Blige were in th
Beyonce and Adele during my drives. Montell Jorda
was doing my hair. I set up a musical army that had

52

ut the day, commercial-free.

me just say there is something truly therapeutic lting "Best Thing I Never Had" by Beyonce like Madison Square Garden with the fans and all. That ught out all types of emotions. I'd cry the first verse, he second, be so empowered I was singing it like owed me money and like my ex was in the crowd from afar.

gs that empower you and play them often. Create onment that allows you to aggressively yell in the ry in the shower, and twerk in a towel. Your playlist y a range of emotions—curate a group of songs that only good memories and vibes. Think of the music getting ready for a girl's night out. Come with that rgy!

y, I don't listen to my anthems as much anymore. still on the playlist, but now when they play, I don't him, our life, or the divorce.

ne of those, "Oh, shit. I haven't heard this in a instead of, "Oh, shit. This fucker really had the to cheat after I accepted that his beard would never "

"DJ, turn that shit up! I'm trying to cry."

Hollywood Fucked Us
Un-romanticize the Idea
of His Ass Coming Back, Ever

Hollywood On a Budget!

Movies, TV, and social media have given us
perception of love, and it sucks. The man who we
to declare his love minutes before your flight is rea
at the bar, watching the game, ordering happy hou
There! I said it. It's a hard pill to swallow, but some
romanticized perception we have of our lives sets
failure. I learned this through others. When I starte
the news with close friends and extended family, I
with many stories of similar experiences, but one
particular, stuck with me to this day.

I knew a couple that was the epitome of #couplego;
had fun together, lived a great life, and were stil
after many years of marriage. I saw a lot of simil
our marriages before the comfort and confusion, anc
that was what I had to look forward to in the future
dust settled.

So, it came as a shock after I told my close friend
affair, and he responded that he and his wife went t
separation after his transgressions. After she found
left the country for work. I asked, "What did you
if there was a light at the end of my matrimonia
Without skipping a beat, he said, "I went and
wife back." He moved to the country where she
refused to leave until she was with him again. They
friends over many months of trying, then started da
eventually got back together.

And just like that, it hit me. Mental snapshot recorc

ah-ha" moment was never going to happen to save
iage, and, most importantly, he didn't want to.

to acknowledge, but realistically, my husband didn't
ave this marriage. From leaving me for seven days
eking couples counseling, he showed me multiple
at he was willing to do, and that was nothing–which
ing devastating.

:ded to acknowledge that I knew the type of person
and while I hoped for the best, my expectations
t realistic. He was never that "move to another
man, so why would I think any adversary would
1: **A.** Grow up overnight or **B.** Be able to take on the
bility of saving our marriage? I looked at the John
and Keanu Reeves of Hollywood and thought that
 me, knowing damn well it wasn't. I had to get real
w my expectations hurt my damn feelings.

inventory of the things he did and started to un-
ize that he would do everything I needed. The
part about looking at situations for what they are
ng your worth to other people's decisions. I did it
ile. Hell! I still do it today, but remember that it's
out you for the most part. My husband's decision
ght for our marriage had nothing to do with me. It
't *in* him. Things might've been different at another
nother situation, but all we had was *this* situation.
ed with what I could control, which was my reaction
happened.

u see the situation for what it is, you can plan a
 reality. The quicker we see actions align with
 traits, we can detach the idea of a Hollywood
ith Prince Charming on a white horse.

reiterate and emphasize that the un-romanticizing
elationship is hard and will hurt your feelings, but

55

his response results from what *he* wanted. I can
Mitchell's "You're So Vain" playing in my mind
never about you, and you eventually learn that's a go
It only needs to be about you on your mother fucking

Helpful ways to get out of Hollywood:

- **Get rid of the "What if?"** Most of the time,
asking, "What if?" because he is not doing wh
expected or thought he would. The more outlan
impossible they seem, the more disappointment y
have.

- **Fantasies come from your imagination.** *A*
wasn't an actual prince, and Cinderella was a mai
not forget, these characters changed with magic. `
love to go to the land of fantasy, but if you're drear
a different action from the same person, it's not r
Look at the source. If they've shown you who th
believe them.

- **Stop making it so easy to hurt your feelings**
expectations, lack of boundaries, overthinkin
allowing people to affect your energy only I
heartache. Stop hurting your damn feelings, gi
have control over your reactions, and that's it. Ins
waiting for him to be that man, buy you those flowe
take you to that place, do it for yourself. Expect I
and reign in your light. It makes the element of s
more special.

- **Know this isn't every relationship.** The failu
relationship is not all relationships. There are mar
respect, love, honesty, openness, etc., and you w
it. Yes, there is a little romanticization in the id
someone would move a mountain for you, but th
person wouldn't feel like it was a mountain, and
want to move it for you.

ered the affair days before Valentine's Day and
multiple offices after realizing he did nothing. Two
ater, on what would've been our second wedding
ary, he sent flowers, chocolate-covered strawberries
s of remorse, and I felt nothing; it was too little, too
in't want him anymore.

t, *"If he wanted to, he would." It's, "He had the
chance and didn't."*

Log Off. Social Media Can See T[...] Hands.

#Sorrynotsorry

Social media is toxic. Aside from the false percepti[...] all shaped like centaurs, it's the accessibility o[...] anyone at any time. When I found out the affair [...] with his coworker, I became obsessed with finding [...] she was. I'd ask myself, "Is she prettier than me? [...] than me?" I assumed it was the truth. So, I sco[...] internet in search of the faceless woman.

I started with the basics: Facebook and Instagram. [...] was very generic, and my husband refused to giv[...] additional information. I'd get on the phone with [...] friend, and we'd search tags, photos, and compani[...] to find a clue, hint, or evidence to take our search to[...] level. We ended up finding nothing, but every fal[...] left me nauseous. I told myself I couldn't keep d[...] shit. I was hurting my feelings.

Not to mention the constant bombardment of our [...] memories together, and how happy everyone [...] around me. It wasted my time and negatively distr[...] from feeling and healing.

Give your mind a break, delete all social media a[...] your phone, limit your screen time, and put yo[...] down. While this can be very hard, keep an app t[...] with the urges to scroll. Pinterest is great because [...] still disconnect from friends (if you don't follow [...] boards), but there's a smorgasbord of information t[...] mentally. Look up self-help-quotes, healthy food [...] lists, interior design ideas, and you'll eventually find [...]

ored and logging off after 10 minutes. Get your fix,
eel good after.

ay off as long as you can. You're not missing a
ng. After a year, I logged back on and saw several
s and messages asking about my hiatus. I responded
about my breakup and got, "I'm sorry to hear," and
ard from them again. Just to show you, people are
curious, and whether you are around to answer or
will always be there.

girl from high school is still selling that expensive
poo, and that one friend just had another baby."

You are A Do-Something Bitch

Girl, you doin' the most and we here for

Do-Something Bitch

[doo; unstressed doo, duh suhm-thing bich]

noun

You: The opposite of a Do-Nothing Bitch.

- A female that is about her shit.
- A go-getter.
- A nasty woman in all aspects of life.
- A woman who continually strives to progress in th
  emotionally, mentally, and physically.
- A woman who minds their own business to build
  own business.

"I don't have time to entertain this. I'm on my Do-S
Bitch *Shit, Vanessa!" Ashley said, after acknowle
hater's ill intentions.*

verb

To strive, progress.

*"She vowed to always be a Do-Something Bitch
midlife crisis."*

Antonym
Do-Nothing Bitch; hater, negative, lazy
Slang. To do nothing.

*"You're acting like a Do-Nothing Bitch after harbo
toxic behavior."*

mething Bitch takes action and decides to succeed in
ts of her life by any means necessary. She's making
ion every day to set herself up for the abundance of
nent that she deserves.

l to pursue a lifelong dream and move to New York

e ballsiest and most drastic thing to do, but I had no
cuses. Making such a change was intimidating, and
once the words "I'm moving" left my mouth, there
going back. I gave the Universe a hint and talked

ne only thing I talked about. "I'm moving to NYC
e comedy writing." There wasn't a conversation
ou didn't know what my plans were and how I would
them. I claimed it. Some dreams should be kept to
, but this tactic made my word bond. I never wanted
er the dreaded "What happened to you moving?"
myself that would never be me. So, I put it into all
of my world as a reminder, then set a date.

1, 2018.

ober deadline was set in February to give me enough
save up money and muster the courage to actually
nce the date was set, I put it in multiple calendars
up a countdown. This was a time to celebrate. I had
onths to save, get a divorce, and find a new job. I
nfidently say it was what I wanted, but I was scared
Then, I worked my ass off.

or Do-Something's to remember:

those goodies. Goodies can come in the form of
al independence, mental clarity, or even your
al body. Remember, all of these actions are

temporary and meant to help you progress into th
chapter of your Do-Something Bitch livelihood.

• **Hustle.** You never want money to be the reaso
you didn't go for it, so don't let it. Two jobs, O
Something Bitch. Financial independence is som
necessary for success on your "that bitch" crusade.
a side hustle or second job to supplement that neec

• **A Goal in Mind (emphasis on *mind*).** If you
exactly sure where to start, ask yourself, "what a
good at?" Or specifically, "What do you want to b
at?" Everything is attainable, but you have to kno
you want. So, get creative!

• **Move that bawdy!** Go for a walk, take a workou
get physical. It's the easiest and most natural thi
can do. Let those endorphins answer some of your
questions.

• **There's a Downside to Comfort.** Comfort
difference between you and the people around y
all hear, "I wish that I did this when I could," or,
I would've given to have that opportunity again."
small, there is such importance in picking a person
and sticking to it. Aside from it taking your mind
everything going on, it just reminds you of how m
a Do-Something Bitch you are. Don't pick comfo
will regret it. The only comfort you should acc
crocs, laying on clean sheets, and giving up heels f
Das it!

So, I did it.
Because, why the fuck not?

The art of being a Do-Something Bitch is acknowlec
already who you are. It was you before your marria
your divorce, during college, training for that n

our hair with dull scissors, taking that girl's trip,
having dinner by yourself watching *The Sopranos*.

"You're already the masterpiece."

Things Do-Something Bitches Do:

Eat
Sleep
Beast shit
Kill shit
Repeat

Things Do-Nothing Bitches Do:
Eat
Project
Talk shit
Sleep
Repeat

See the difference? Know the difference.

Believe All the Hype.
ɔok At That Coochie in the Tub.

ɪhale that ass and exhale everything else."

ɛ of years into my marriage, I gained around 35
ɪnd stopped giving a fuck about myself. I would cry
ɪe. My husband would come home to me crying on
for no particular reason. He'd ask, "What's wrong?"
ɪldn't answer because I didn't know why either. It
lowest I'd ever felt, and this was with all societal
ɪons met; marriage, friends, and a damn good job.

ɪt, a group of girlfriends wanted to go out and
ɪ had nothing to wear because nothing fit. One of the
ɛlings to look in the mirror and relive that Regina
ɪoment in *Mean Girls* of, "Sweatpants are the only
ɪt fits me right now." A physical representation of
ɛssion, I looked in the mirror with half-open jeans
ɪis was rock bottom. My skin was a wreck, and my
undone. I made little-to-no effort to care about how
or how I wanted to feel.

ɔrce, I started my journey to figure out self-care.

y, when you're at the lowest place in life, a lot of
ɪst recommend a bubble bath or reading a book, as if
ɪporary feelings would provide the deeper meaning
vhat it is that's hurting you and how to fix it. So, I
'here I was familiar: Pinterest.

attempt included hours on Pinterest and google
for self-care suggestions. I'd take baths, buy myself
play music, sing, meditate, read, etc. At first, it was
. I'd draw a bath, and after a couple of minutes,

I'd get in and sit there like, "What now? Watch the
disintegrate into my coochie hair?" I'd burn up
being too hot and just take a shower. I'd light candl
favorite scent and let it burn for a bit, then blow
I need the fire hazard? My toes looked like sneak
sneakers), but did I need to get the pedicure acco
with awkward eye contact foot massage?

The answer was yes. Yes, bitch. Do it all.

Over time, the evolution of having conversations
coochie and eye contact with my pedicurist tur
things I looked forward to during the week. I'd foun
picking a night in over getting tanked at some dingy
coworkers. Yes, those times were great, but I lost
of Missing Out (FOMO). I didn't worry about eve
wasn't doing when I was content at home with mys

My takeaway from self-care is faking the smushy
things until it becomes a habit, and you love it.

Self-care=Self-love.

You watch trash TV, drink a glass of wine, buy pla
be so busy with shit that makes you feel good
eventually start to love a part of yourself. It will hap
not overnight. Say it with me, "Consistency is key
comes to loving me." Cheesy, but true. This is also
when you get to the monotonous side of self-care.

Unlike the movies and social media, self-love and
be boring if it's not personalized to you. It's not
cliche line of, "Dance like no one's watching." Rea
no one dances in the living room unless it's for a
The more specific it is to you, the more beneficia
You don't like baths, save the coochie conversations
vibrator. You can't keep a plant alive? Papier Mac
Everything used to make you feel good has to be

:o what you like. If not, it'll become routine and
ıd creative ways to spend your time, and if you're
 get, spice it up! Try new nail colors, incorporate
 scrubs, or switch up your coffee to iced. You have
 t work for you.

ve patience with yourself, especially when you
. Any effort toward being only about yourself will
 result in choosing yourself over everything else.
:ady.

ıon-bath lovers or appreciators of a new skincare
Here are small ways you can start to practice self-

to yourself positively in the mirror. (And yes, it
mfortable.) Side note: It's almost as uncomfortable
n you squat down in front of a mirror to see what
agina looks like. Words of advice, proceed with
.

ıge in little shit. flowers for your home, art, knick-
, or coffee from a local shop in the morning. Think
he small, inexpensive things that make you feel
ıay is going to be "okay."

an effort to shower. I personally used to put my
 a bun and not do shit for the rest of the day. The
is true; if you make an effort to look good, you will
ılly feel good or smell good.

your bedsheets. Rid yourself of the last cry and
ky ass. If you live alone, still do it. It's time.

people who make you smile or feel good about
lf. Get your mind off of yourself.
al and make lists of goals or a to-do list. The key
) old school, using pen and paper. Once finished,

you can turn the page, burn the page, or refer back
future. You will find clarity.

Now, I can continue with the list, but you get th
doesn't have to be the most prominent expression
you feel good. Recognize what you want with inter
don't give a fuck what others think. If you want
dozen cookies, eat them. If you want to spend n
those shoes, get them. Now, also be sensible. We
out here like some beautiful, happy, self-loving, b
bitches, but that's just how it is. Self-love includes
things. Self-love, self-centeredness, self-understand
in the end, self-control is all toward the betterment

Get used to being by yourself, and one day you w
that ah-ha moment of "I'm okay" and not just an "
without him or the relationship." More of an "I'm
and present" type of "okay." I gave up everything
was married, putting my own love after my ex-husb
house, job, and other distractions. So now, pickin
seemed only natural.

A few notes once before you start:

I had a friend tell me, "You just have to do it until yo
it." The more you do the things that make you feel g
easier it is. You will slowly become an expert.

Don't let Pinterest intimidate you into not doing
beneficial for ideas, but toxic positivity is a real th
not everyone is living in an NYC penthouse ap
drinking fresh-pressed juice, and meditating in
expensive pair of Lululemon leggings.

If it makes you feel like a trash can, it's not self-
self-destruction. Don't drain your energy by add
others' expectations.

icator if you're in the act of self-love, or learning
ss, is asking, and answering: *How do I feel when I*
_?

positive or fulfilling, move on.

s someone is great but pooping with the door open
ing a whole pizza on a Friday night is great too."

Do the *Do*.

"It scared me, so I did it anyway."

I am a firm believer that things will eventua
themselves out. It might look and feel different, but
respond will determine the outcome. Realistically,
have a choice, right? The Universe does whatever
she wants but letting her know you're ready helps
the decision.

The mindset of *Do*.
The hardest obstacle to completing your goals is ma
a *healthy* mindset. The emphasis is on *healt*
"positive" can sometimes be unrealistic. Feelings,
and your state of mind can change by the second.
doesn't always mean joyous, zippy, and excit
everything in your life. A healthy mindset is ado
mentality of knowing you're always going to be
picking yourself up when shit sucks. It's reminding
that feelings are temporary and that you decide to h
and bad days. It's taking a break and recognizing th
for the course. Once the mind is healthy, obstac
way of the *Do* have workarounds, different courses
and positive redirection.

The action of *Do*.
This will be easy. We all have different timeline
emphasis of *Do* is getting that ass up and active
steps towards what you want. If you're a late bl
(like me) impatient as hell to get it done, time doesn
The pace at which you decide is completely fine. T
of the *Do* is you decide when conversations wil
deposits will be made, and memberships are cancel
you've figured out what you want and how to g

make that shit happen. There's no turning back on
he change to giving yourself an abundance of what
ve: happiness.

est decision in life is taking control of it.
again.

ow the *Do* is scary, like walking alone down an
 in Michael Myers's neighborhood type of scary
ng is scarier. Live your life like the shit you repost
ram and the corny posters you have in your office.
ly, laugh uncontrollably, and love yourself enough
t you've been talking about.

*re is power in declaring it and holding yourself
accountable for it."*

Nikki Frias

Trust the Universe. She Stays Loyal.

Frankie never lies.

Frank Sinatra's music has brought back a form of
One particular memory was singing "Fly Me to Th
while cooking dinner with my dad during the sum
kid. Not played commonly on the playlist in rece
one evening Frank Sinatra gave me a sign that pus
go for my dreams.

My October deadline was approaching, and I w
shitless. When it was heavy on my mind, I'd talk to
verse. I assume she's bold, beautiful, and always
listen when I want to get things off my chest. I'd as
making the right decision moving? Can I do this?"

Later that day, my phone synced up to my car, and
dora started to play:

It's up to you, New York, NEWWW YOORRRKKK

I sat in awe. The Universe had spoken. Before that
spirituality and I have had an on-again, off-again rela

A non-religious person, I assumed the Universe an
Nature were cousins. I believed in her and knew
there, but like, "Bitch, where have you been?" We k
other but never spoke. I had friends who were into
spirituality, astrology, and they'd always say, "Ma
but I couldn't grasp the concept. You want me just t
it, and it'll work out? Girl, what?

:lieve the Universe had my back. Some of the ways
ayed it were very harsh. I mean, I was getting a
living in my mother's home, had an unfulfilling
am now lactose intolerant. If this was her way of
ne I made the right decision, I didn't want to know
she had in store. I was cautious, but what did I
se?

verything else. I needed answers.

ied a "How-To" guide and couldn't find much, but
retation of manifesting is a physical representation,
er, an idea, or positive thought that leads you to
a goal. It's giving yourself the best possibility to
goal through action. Write it down, talk about it like
ly here, and everything around you will respond.

ies:

it down and use post-It notes. Write down blurbs
you want and place them everywhere. Try to be
ific as possible. When I say everywhere, I mean
here: cars, desk, mirror, computer, back of my cell
purse–you name it. The constant reminders keep
track and focused on the bigger picture. Right
y post-it says, "New York Times Best Seller."

ositive affirmations. I found one online and set
der on my phone. "I don't chase. I only attract.
s made for me will find me." After a while, try
orize it, and eventually say it daily or at 11:11.
nt to cover all bases. When you're saying your
tions, be sure to close your eyes and envision the
u want, whether it be a man, a house, a job, etc.

ccordingly. Plan the goal like it's already in place
e your actions reflect it. For me, when manifesting
downsized my things, looked up places to visit,

applied for jobs, and started apartment shopping
small steps towards what you see for your future.

• **Be consistent.** Consistency shows how bad you
especially when you don't think she's listening.

• **Listen to the Universe.** She has a lot to say
realizing the Universe has your back, she can
talking. The signs, clues, opportunities, and rer
constantly push you in the right direction. The hir
there all along. You just weren't ready to receive t

Now, this goes without saying, but my interpre
manifestation came from talking with friends
searches, and developing my ideology through my pe
We all have different wants, needs, and expectatie
that, I recommend doing your research to figure or
means to you. Manifesting has many layers and
but only you can define its capabilities. All that to s
manifesters and spiritual advisors, don't come for :

I can hear her now. "We could've avoided all this s
pain, Nikki!" You started to believe you were des
all the things you wanted, and it began to show u
emphasis on *you*.

My decision to move my life to another city
aggressive for a newbie. Still, I did it with plannin
realistic expectations, and most importantly, no
back on myself.

"The Universe talks to you. You just need to lis.

Yes! Let That Inner Werk.

xa! Play "Me, Myself and I" by Beyonce.

noved to NYC, I struggled with my happiness.
to popular belief, moving to a new place doesn't
ally give you a new life. My divorce was old news,
I was left alone to overthink, replay, and replace
as the best times of my life. There were no more
ns, and after the dust settled, I had to figure out how
forward alone. This time there wasn't a person to
a situation to address with a partner. I was holding
countable for where I was in life.

revert to what I learned in therapy, but it only
the surface of my inner work. Inner work can be
uncomfortable to dig deep, seek meaning, and
ne trauma linked to some failed parts of ourselves.
ich easier to ignore, but everything changes once
better perception of yourself. You, your energy, your
ns, your standards, all that shit. The divorce forced
to the next chapter, but now I needed to grow from
a.

arned from Inner work:

quires consistent effort. Inner work involves a
motional effort. You have to actively find these
within yourself through self-reflection, therapy,
stant work toward your progress.

o your fears. What's the fear, and why is it scary
ess? Is this situation something you can't avoid? If
are you avoiding it? Confront those emotions and
the hard questions. Most of the time, your feelings

conjure up a false narrative of a person or percep
situation. We all villainize people and situations
make us anxious. Take back the power and contr
you can. If you pinpoint where your fears are
from, it's a lot easier to see where they're rooted.

For example, I noticed many fears stemmed fror
single and finding new love after my divorc
was I so scared to be alone? What happened in
that created this perception that minimal love h
accepted? Ironically, I was no longer interested i
or anything that came with it, but I knew these
issues needed to be addressed for me ever to feel

- **Self-Awareness is a game-changer.** How yo
interpret, and communicate with others allows
to be honest around you. So much of what you
about yourself comes from not being defensive (
typical for me) and listening to how you are pe
by your closest people. It's a hard pill to swallow,
incredibly beneficial. Remember, it's a privilege
people around you willing to be honest about h
make them, or others, feel. The friend that tells yc
the shit in your teeth, keep them.

- **The way you talk to yourself matters.** We ar
best at talking to ourselves. Addressing your body
but the mental and emotional can be awkward.
noticed how bad it was until my best friend sai
aren't very nice to yourself." She was right. If y
attention, the way you talk or don't talk about yo
very telling of how you feel about yourself. If yo
comfortable with it, try to make a list of what
accomplished to review and remind yourself just
you've come.

- **When you feel most down or fearful, write i**
Write everything down. I will continuously say t

ficial. When you have negative thoughts, take
utes, and write down all the worst outcomes
atever holds you back. I know, this sounds super
us, but surprisingly it is effective. I tried this when
erwhelmed by possible negative outcomes in life,
iend recommended I just put it all on paper. After
utes, you will see the reality of your thoughts and
ot is conjured up from overthinking.

ed to see how your brain works on paper. Seeing
ike "abandoned" and sayings like, "My life will
ave meaning" shows a visual representation of how
your thoughts can be. After a couple of minutes,
d I struggled to write out more negative, untrue
and unintentionally started responding to my self-
e. I'd say to myself, "I can never be abandoned
I have X" and "I've already accomplished X and
h have meaning."

imes you do suck, but we all do. There are times
e all suck. Whether you've put your foot in your
had malicious thoughts, or even did something
ely out of character, you're not alone. Forgive
f for whatever it is. The only person that needs
to terms with your behavior is you. Sit with the
assing, intolerable, and upsetting actions you've
and learn to make the situation better by how
dle future incidents or how to respond. The root
issues will always be with you.

vas just a catalyst to finally seeking the answers, and
rs never stop. I should also note that inner growth
s. You either maintain to reach a comfortable level
, or you let that shit go and allow the comfort of
less in all aspects of your life to seep right back
universe. Change is hard, and it's also really
cary. I get it, but there is no greater feeling than
hat the silence you once feared is a sign of peace

instead of loneliness.

*"I can't wait for the day you recognize your peace,
you prioritize yourself, your energy, and pay attention to
how people make you feel."*

Romanticizing Mr. Frias

he's making a list and checking it twice!

dating would be a repeated cycle of disappointment
st. I'd meet someone, notice the red flags, try to
ork, and it would eventually end with a new bullet
sband list. It started to be a waste of time and a
1 from my personal goals.

a lot of things to the Universe. My future husband
added to the list. I made a conscious effort to find
nd have completely burned out on dating. No one
at how emotionally draining dating with intention
I had to hold in another fart during the talking
was going to explode (literally.) I've talked with
men who found love after their "practice marriage,"
them searched, wrote down, or even prayed for
re husbands. So, moving forward, I am declaring
future husband until he meets me at the altar.

own the qualities I want in my next relationship,
n the basics of loyalty, honesty, and respect:

onally available.
nunicative.
rtive.
ethic.
ady, sneaky games, unless it's Candy Crush. I
even like to go through my own phone.
nizes my light and doesn't try to dim it.
dividual goals and actively works toward them.
to the idea of eating everything bagel seasoning
git everything.
ike dogs. It says a lot about a person.

- Is Present.
- Not materialistic.
- Patient, especially with my ass.
- Not weird about body hair, especially during co
  seasons.

Interestingly enough, when I reread my list, I
wrote "recognizes my self-worth" as a require
realized that I struggled with my self-worth. I'm w
it, but unlearning is a process, especially when, hi
I've tied my worth to a man.

Giving the responsibility of trust to the Universe
the opportunity to focus on manifesting the goals t
gives you a chance to refocus and slow down once
something, or someone is doing the work. Distra
always be there, and it can be hard to maintain, but
to remind myself:

> **Time is inconsequential.** Moments are mom
> doesn't matter how long you've been with som
> have a connection. We all have that one friend th
> her man, and they've been rocking since high sch

> **Fuck societal norms.** Your Mr. Frias might
> infertile, previously divorced apple of my ey
> he might be missing an eye, but he will be eve
> I've ever hoped for in a spouse. Just because y
> timelines and expectations, it's out of your contro

> **There is a difference between being alone and**
> One is a state of being. The other is a feeling.

Figure out what you want, need, and like about
Mr. Frias, and yes, he will have your last name fo
of smashing the patriarchy. When you didn't kn

ed, you accepted anything. Make a list of your
s and expectations as a favor to your feelings and
d refer to it when you think you've met the one.
ur non-negotiables in pen or permanent marker.
e them originally with purpose. Don't try to erase
! If he goes against a non-negotiable, take time to
e and determine why you're willing to budge now
person. Figure out your limitations and boundaries
meone decides them for you.

> *"If you want me to take you seriously,*
>   *you need to come serious."*

Oh, and Another Thing: Forgive Already!

*Out of all the chapters, this one took the lon;
write and is the most sincere.*

Forgiveness is weird. It's not something you wal
morning and, bam, you're whole again. It takes
work, self-reflection, and creating your meaning o
My closure was letting go of the idea that time mea
and the importance of my self-worth in relations
don't get it twisted. There have been times when
to myself over the fact that he had someone, a
making small talk over cold spinach and artichok
even single and alone, I wouldn't want it any othe

Throughout my divorce, I was never vengeful o
figured being negative in a time when I was most v
would only mean it'd take longer to heal. I look
those ten years and sometimes forget it ever happe
I was another person, in another life, and that's t
was.

That 18-year-old girl is unrecognizable compared
am today. Through my healing, growth, and unde
I was able to control the narrative for the first ti
fucking life. The decision was made for me, bu
forced me to actively choose myself and deal wi
shit that came with that.

When growing through the process of forgivene
notice some things are expected, and others come
territory.

:aways from the lessons include:

accountability. There were times when you
the most supportive, understanding, and loving
o, you didn't deserve any of what happened, but
) have to take accountability for the hurtful and
things you've said and done. You didn't get to
nt out of just anywhere. At one point or another,
th stopped nurturing and contributing to the
ship's success, and it needs to be acknowledged.

mber, they're human. Shit happens. People fuck
decision was selfish, but that was one of his flaws,
as to live with it.

take it personally. For the most part, it has
to do with you. Projection is real.

esn't Require the Other Person. Closure party
Adding another person to your healing leaves you
d and hopeful of an alternate ending.

veness is a slow process. It happens in stages.
periences and conversations you never thought
appen do, and it starts to hurt less. Do the work of
, and eventually, moments will happen to remind
our progress.

as April 27, 2017. I got a text saying, "I know today
" from my now ex-husband on what would've been
wedding anniversary. The significance of that day
by like a missed dentist appointment.

ss is an everyday process. I repeat, an everyday
until one day, major holidays don't suck, and
has to remind you of the life you used to have.

time heals all wounds, and dammit, they (whoever)

were correct. It's hard but necessary to move on
life. Divorce forces you to make a change, but fc
allows you to enjoy the journey of what that chan
Damn! That's some Oprah-type shit.

To my ex-husband: I sincerely hope you're well, a
you well.

Let me say it louder for the people in the back:

"Divorce forces you to make a change, but forg
allows you to enjoy the journey of what that change

Chapter Five:
d Now a Trip to the
and of Misfit Toys!

"Split checks, please!"

Hey, U Up?
Remain calm and swipe on!

My experience with dating before my marriage w
skim. I went on a couple of dates, and after
conversation over first date food like chicken te
salads, I met my husband. For most of my 20's, I
relationship. I never had the quintessential "hoe
time just to dick around (literally).

Fast forward to dating at 28, I had different expecta
requirements for dating. It didn't start with a "W
and finish with a "I'm not ready for a relationshi
I decided to take the plunge after considering the
factors:

• Dating gives you a reason to dress up a little
than the usual legging and sweatshirt ensemble. Th
excitement of finding that $9.99 Forever 21 ou
getting ready for a night is worth it.

• It gives you the experience to learn what you are
and not willing to accept when dating someone n

• Dating shows you more about yourself; how you
with others, your openness, and your boundari
new people.

• It reminds you that romance isn't dead, flirting
and an opportunity for butterflies is exciting.

• And most importantly, you're not alone. Many
are looking for love and potentially want it to be w

So, get to swiping and have fun. Just remember

ıgs. We've all ignored a flag or two, but we can't
ɩarning from the future to be ignored over the fear
alone. Red flags are blessings because they show
<ly not to waste your time, effort, or energy on a
ɩo doesn't deserve you. When the Universe gives
ɩ of what you don't need, listen to her.

ɩumb: red flags mean run.

ɪiled attempts at love have developed a list of tell-
to have your sneakers ready. It should be noted: if
at this list and compare the person you're dating,
ɩat closet and grab em'. It's race day.

ɩn't text you the first date address until he gets
cks Wi-Fi, **RUN.**
go to his house and he hands you basketball shorts
r, **DASH.**
okay with you slipping a $15 check on a first date,
ˀ.
ɩakes fun of anything about you within the first
ɩ of months, **SCURRY.**
s over the age of 38 and still renting, **SCAMPER.**
try to introduce him to new food like brie and he's
about it, **FLY.**
ɔalls all the women he's encountered "crazy,"
ˀ.
weird about new experiences or country music,
D WALK.
ɩas no friends, **BOOK IT, BITCH.**
ɔver says, "I'm afraid I might be too big," before
ɔ had sex, **BOLT.**
ɩys things like "You women" or "Let my guess,
ɩ a feminist?" **WHIZ.**
ɔwns or rents a Dodge Charger, **ACCELERATE**
˘ **TOE-TO-HEEL RANGE.**
email address makes a reference to money or a
ɩe post-2007, for example, "moneyrunner127@

gmail.com" or "imthatboi88@yahoo.com",
SKEDADDLE.
- If he changes his voice when he's on the phone ·
mother, **CLEAR OUT.**
- If he eats his scabs or hair, **MARATHON RUN I
MARATHON.**
- If he always keeps his phone on Do Not Disturb
GALLOP LIKE SEABISCUIT.
- If he litters, even the most minor thing, **MOVE
IT'S THE TIMED MILE IN 5th GRADE PE**
- If he wants you to meet his family after the third
VAMOOSE.
- If he doesn't own a suit or a collared shirt, **STA**
LEG ON OUT.
- If he wears jeans with designs on them, from embr
roses to bleach designs, **EXPEDITE THAT AS**
- If he gets intimidated by your personal goals and ·
FUCK RUNNING, FLY.
- If he doesn't brush his teeth before bed, **BECO**
SUPERHERO AND FLASH!
- If he doesn't clip his toenails with clippers, but ▮
300m SPRINT.
- If he doesn't have a wallet or money clip,
AGGRESSIVELY WALK AWAY.

And now off to the whimsical land of disappoint▮
dating life.

Please note: this segment is for entertainment purp
they are real stories, and yes, some information
changed, so a bitch doesn't get sued. I hope you
journey of dating these men as much as I enjoyed
them. Cheers!

Rule #1: Never settle due to convenience. You will eventually lose yourself.

The Ex-Husband.

n why we're all here.

thing about dating someone at 18 is all you do is ward sex and eat out a lot. Looking back, we didn't t about each other, and we were also opposites, but ked Red Lobster biscuits, so I thought we'd at least obster Fest.

on many dates and had a lot of experiences, but elt like we knew one another, we didn't. We had ly different likes and interests, and eventually, comfortable living separate lives together that it ur reality.

Universe started early with the lessons, she gave rst red flag in the relationship before I even knew d flag was. Our first date was dinner at Friday's and o see *The Pursuit of Happiness*.

were at dinner, a girl came up and asked if he was other girl. It's as if the Universe was screaming at bitch! This is a red flag! Leave, and don't look ut I just sat quietly and feasted on my Friday's hicken and cheese.

ne I'm getting divorced at 28 and now being put the "dating scene" years later without a fucking to navigate it. Some lessons were learned. Some some hard. But it forced introspection in a way say I will be ready for Mr. Frias. If he doesn't ever still be okay.

Red Flags
Unmotivated.
Cheater.

Misfit Tip
Relationships that stand the test of time are notabl
of the amount of work they require. Falling in
sometimes push us into situations that aren't ide
long haul, so knowing your limitations can red
heartache. Before getting into a relationship, make
know yourself and your boundaries. Establish
want in a partner and be vocal about expectation
yourself first makes loving someone else so mu
Time waits for no one. So, if it's not working, w
because one minute you're sharing fondue on V
Day, and the next you're sleeping in separate bed
of his sleep apnea.

You can get tired. Take a break, but don't ever giv

Rule #2: People can come into your life,
ge it, and things still don't work out.

The Wokeness.

e Wokeness on the couch at my close friend's
. It was the first time I'd ever met a person I had
connection with. I kid you not, we locked eyes,
s like we had known one another for years. The
ion was consistent, energy was on 1000, and it was
spoken understanding we both felt at that moment.
committed relationship with my now ex-husband,
vening, I forgot. The rest of the evening was us
ancing salsa, and laughing. When I got home that
ld my then boyfriend, now ex-husband, I met The
, and it was a great time. Unphased, life went on.

new it, this was a definite red flag about my current
ip. I never forgot The Wokeness even years later.
ard to my separation, I wanted to feel good, texted
we ended up dating a couple of months later.

p for a date, and the chemistry was as if we never
he following year included dinner by candlelight,
aths together, laughter, and a lot of vulnerable
. He came up to see me when I moved to NYC and
me throughout my divorce; it was what I needed.
y great love story, we mutually decided not to be
fter about a year of dating.

ately, we disagreed on moral values and, while I
ut him deeply, the life I wanted for myself looked
rent for him. The Wokeness taught me a lot about
d showed me the type of love I never knew I needed
notional love.

For those who haven't met their version of The
emotional love entailed accepting others' feeling
partners accountable, and understanding the labo
It is a lot of work, and I was not in the busines
then. This was not why we broke up, but there
of growing pains throughout the relationship. I c
back and say that The Wokeness made me a be
partner, and spouse to my future husband. He g
lot of patience and understanding, which at the
intimidating.

I would say that while I know my husband is out
was never to love again, I would be okay after h
emotional experiences I did with this man; it wa
Ironically, out of all the other missed encounters,
only one that is still considered a good friend.
has changed but experiencing a different type of
divorce showed me it was possible.

It follows the saying, "What one man won't dc
will." The Wokeness made me look forward to a fu
that included what I wanted and more.

Red Flag
Different lifestyles.

Misfit Tip
Love is necessary, but the success of a relationshi
so much more than emotions. The initial chemist
what connects you, but it isn't what keeps you. Wh
that partner, make sure your values in the relatio
aligned, or else it'll turn into another lesson. Iron
beauty in the lesson is how much it shows you abou
Be receptive to learning about the negative parts y
your relationship. It will make you a better partn
future.

Rule #3: Never fuck someone from your
, and if he has an Android, nope. I'm not
king about the green bubbles and lack of
ɔ. That Android is some sort of witchcraft;
ol' stalking my stalking ass.

The Coworker.

ıt my first ever retail job, and I learned quickly
should never shit where you eat or shit in the same
someone who knows where you sleep. It started
when he was restocking the candy aisle, and I was
g bread. No, but seriously. We texted a couple of
our first date was at a cute restaurant one night
k.

was fine; beautiful body, face, lips.

d for a couple of months, and he was fun, but I
known what our future entailed after dinner on
late. We went to a random park in Manhattan, and
d questions like, "What do you think of me?" after
ow to pronounce his real name two hours earlier.
nade out that entire night and, while I wasn't ready,
ith it. We had sex a couple of dates later. It was
ling I had and the first time I'd experienced non-
sex. Sorry mom and dad, the cat's out of the bag.
n'.

I enjoyed the non-emotional when he threw me
ke a rag doll, but it slowly faded. Over time, I didn't
ave sex anymore because of the emptiness I felt
t forward a couple of weeks later, things quickly
oxic once his temper mixed with my nonchalant
to most situations.

The worst thing after we ended was I had to see ▯
day. He had a way to pick at me and push my ▯
firmly believe everyone has a breaking point, and h▯
right after my G-spot. His behavior was cyclical. ▯
instigate a fight, have an outburst, and block me. T▯
of toxic behavior was making me no better than hi▯
draining and brought me to a level of Patty. One i▯
was blocked and, after what I assumed was the 1▯
decided to put the phone down.

Days later, he finally answered one of my calls.

ring...ring...
Him: Hi Nikki.
Me: "Oh, hey! I just figured I'd give you a call aft▯
conversation."
Him: "I know."
Me: "You know what?"
Him: "You called me 16 times, Nikki. Android tell▯
Me: "Oh, that's awkward."
Who knew Android tells you how many times ▯
number calls you? I would take the bait every t▯
admittedly, this man had me out here looking like t▯
of Cut-a-Bitch town. The humiliation helped my a▯
and it was the last time I talked to him.

It was dreadful. I eventually quit and avoided hir▯
plague. Like most men, I got an email months lat▯
how I was. Yawn.

Red Flags
Intense rage over small things.
Hated my dog.
Awkward around groups of people.
A strange sense of humor, like cringy.
Made jokes out of my vulnerabilities.
Accidentally called me his ex-girlfriend's name tw▯

p

o get swept up in the idea of meeting a significant
work but understand the ramifications. Yes, it's
ess around, but that good dick might be attached
path that enjoys toxic situationships. If you find
slipping into a similar destructive level, it's time
out mentally, emotionally, and physically on aisle

Dating Rule #4: If he doesn't understan women act the way they do, he is the pr Emotional intelligence is a make or bre relationships.

The Infamous Fuck Boy.

Fuck Boys are like sitcoms; they don't last that lor meant to entertain.

Disclaimer: The Fuck Boy can come in multipl sizes, and definitions. While some think the desc a Fuck Boy is just a guy who only wants to fuck, come to distract, annoy, and leave you confused. F their style, piercings, haircut, nice body, and humo all meant to waste your time. While not all the s can see them grazing on dating websites, bars, a parks alike.

I thought Fuck Boys were a rare breed since I tru had any experience with them until I met my first F in NYC on Tinder. So, I think before we start, w have a moment of silence for how fucking fine this Like, bow your head. This man was fine. The typ that you're surprised you bagged him your damn was a confidence boost of "damn bitch, you got inner self.

We texted a little and shared occasional phone c boom, a dick pic with a "How are you?" text. For c first official Fuck Boy DPs, it was slightly underw Position, 3; small bathroom, -3; dick, 6.5. I mean, going to send me a naked picture before the showe at least focus on the lighting? Like kryptonite, the he had was humor.

of a great Fuck Boy is humor, and he was fucking
We talked for a week or so until he told me he
ed a good time. While I respected it, and later
it, I told him that wasn't my vibe and declined. We
d a friendship for a couple of months after I told
wouldn't go out with him unless it was something
y more serious, and he understood. Until one day,
me.

els, assuming the seriousness of the evening, and
ely regretted my decision after walking from the Q
he stairs to the restaurant. I got there a little early
him walking across the street to meet me. He was
and handsome. It was one of the first time's I was
ck by a man. His beautiful ass walked across the
d everyone noticed. I was instantly nervous. We
eet Chick in Brooklyn and sat at a table outside.

r, the conversation was about him being in
on and how the spray paint lines signify something
cians. Who knew? He talked a lot about himself
mpted me to ask, "Do you only talk about yourself?"
l, and the conversation finally transitioned to more
th of us could contribute to. Just when the vibe
ng better, he hit me the most Fuck Boy of Fuck
tions. "This is like a friend's date, right?" And just
ladies, I'd been tricked! Not sure how to respond,
ou should've fucking told me that before I wore
ddly, after the awkward interaction, the rest of the
it seamlessly. We ended up getting doughnuts and
the steps of the Brooklyn Museum talking about
hings like animals and inventions. It was Taylor
gwriting-type shit if she was raised in Brooklyn.

tarted to get late, he dropped me off at my apartment,
ited him up. The chemistry was pretty spot on, but
myself and retracted the invite. Even as beautiful
, I wasn't ready to have sex, and best believe, sex

would've happened that night. He walked me to m[...]
door, and I went inside.

We texted through the night, and I woke up to[...]
morning" text the next day.

Contrary to popular belief, "good morning" te[...]
something. I'm tired of having this argument [...]
about how it's not that big of a deal. It is! Sendin[...]
morning" text shows that person was thinking o[...]
that person wants you to know they're thinkin[...]
Look, there's a shit ton of people that go through [...]
in the morning, and I never text them. Why? Becau[...]
want to see their genitals!

Not trying to overthink it; I went with the flow an[...]
this beautiful dick pic-sending, strong, strappin[...]
nice to me. I can't lie, it was nice. We talked co[...]
for a couple of days, and I started to think I was th[...]
woman to make this Fuck Boy finally change [...]
The progression of feelings led me to build a w[...]
eventually told him "If you have no intentions of ev[...]
me, stop being so nice to me," to which he didn't u[...]
and became cold. I knew these feelings were temp[...]
realistically, it would end up with me multiple te[...]
grievances after four shots of tequila, which is exa[...]
happened. He eventually called me "crazy," and [...]
him.

Red Flags
Cut up light blue jeans with a Bob Marley t-shirt.
Wore sunglasses inside.
Called all past women "crazy."

Misfit Tip
Dating emotionally unavailable men only leads t[...]
coaster of confusion. The danger of a good Fuc[...]
they will tell you what you want to hear and nev[...]

)nce you start to notice a misalignment of actions,
The only woman he will ever love is his mother.
r, he's not here for a long time, just a good time.
:d as such.

Dating Rule #5: Some people will see yo and try to do everything in their power to

That Toxic Ex: Brooklyn Love.

We can all admit we've had that one ex that w
never hear from, bump into, or see for the rest of
That was my Brooklyn Love relationship. The tu
relationship of dating an actual narcissist. Not only
abusive relationship, but the one that reminded m
all relationships require closure or are even necess

I met Brooklyn Love after swearing off men, and v
random Girl's Trip, he slid into my DMs. My initia
of Brooklyn Love were that he seemed nice but
my humor, and we had different interests.

After a couple of flirtatious texts, I said, "What are
tonight?" and smoothly, he responded with, "Waiti
girl I want to take out to go on a date with me." V
my favorite ramen spot and, after that, we had a dr
ready for the evening to end. I had hit my social
the night, but it was only the beginning. That nigl
get home until about 4 AM. Brooklyn Love and I b
and eventually ended up in a SoHo bar basement ki
holding hands. I would say it was very unexpected
I got home, and we quickly became inseparable s
On our second date, I held on to him the entire nigl
was smitten.

After the third or fourth date, the gifts started con
designer jackets to gourmet dinners. I felt like I v
swept off my feet. I had never experienced dating
before, courting like this before and I quickly fell i

nths after we started dating, he moved in.

•: Before anyone comes for me, don't worry, my
d friends already did the job of questioning. Yes,
was fucking crazy, but my logic at that time was
hance. Hell, I spent six years dating the same man
nd tragically. Why not give this new man a chance
vely making an effort to be that man in my life, a
a supporter, etc. Why not? In hindsight, I realize
ess this decision was.

drinking and anger started, completely changing
looked at love.

s a time before he moved in when I should've
e drinking would be a problem, but I was so in
I made excuses as to why it happened. Little did I
t was who he was, and not the man I fell in love
er the next year and a half, I dealt with temper
explosive episodes, property damage, and, I
y, but some physical aggression. I was knee-deep
ationship with an unpredictable narcissist and the
me bomb of eruption left me tense daily. It was
unate circumstance of him refusing to leave that I
was dumb, but I didn't have many options living
by myself and not having many places to run. The
in my name, and it was my responsibility. I also
out the idea of bringing some of my male family to
out, but that also wasn't a viable option seeing the
still had to leave, and well, he knew where I stayed.
ed it up.

ntil a couple of months were left on my lease. I'd
alled a close friend, and she came to get me the
day. I packed a small bag and left with my dog;
needed. I told him I was coming back in a couple
intending to never see him again. Once I got back
ld him he had 30 days to leave. There was no other

way I could do it. He was never going to leave p
ever. So, I did.

I feel like I have processed all that has happened,
get PTSD from situations. It's been hard to proces
thought I'd ever be in a physical altercation with a
when it happened, I struggled as to why I let it hap
I didn't do more, why I stayed. Since then, I ha
to forgive myself and find the silver lining in
happened. There were multiple red flags, but I too
bombing and glam of the situation as authenticity
was not the case.

The silver lining from this situation is that toxic rela
will make you want to never be with another perso
again. A forced relationship can be so bad, so hu
time-consuming. I've had times where I've felt
being single, and I reminded myself that I don
relationship that bad if it is said to be like Brookly

It left scars more hurtful than my divorce.

I thank my lucky stars this was my only encounter
a person, but it also made me super empathetic to
similar situations. It is true what they say. You do
how you'd react until you are knee-deep into the s

And when was the moment that I knew I had to leav
a miscommunication about him using my card, thu
a temper tantrum. I was used to this, but he took
oatmeal and threw it against the wall. It went ev
I was used to it, but the hardest part was seeing m
scared. He was shaking, and that's when I knew th
the lease, all of it didn't matter, and I had to leave.

Red Flag
It's a given.

p

o be guarded and cautious about people's intentions
ing. Pay attention to the signs that you're rushing
thy relationship. Typically, if it seems too good
, it's because it is. Don't misclassify control and
n for "he's really into me." Allow time, space, and
environment for respected boundaries—the little
e excessive drinking and a violent past lead to the
that's never explained.

n an abusive relationship, I pray for you. I know it's
d than done, but block, delete, and do everything in
er to get away from that person. From someone on
side, the fear of sleep will go away, and you will be

ve again without it being so painful.

Dating Rule #6: Lack of communicatior he's married, or he ain't about that l

The Potentially Married Man.

Mr. Potentially Married and I had a couple of r
dating until I concluded his lack of communicatior
to his wife. Now, the verdict is not out, but I assum
the case.

We went on a couple of dates and talked pretty of
noticed communication was sparse during the wee
thinking anything of it, I would assume he was
we'd pick up during the week, until it was blatant
lived a double life. I had to exit stage right. I mear
out of town every weekend and would only talk to
hours. Clearly, there was something else going on.

I texted him, "This isn't enough for me, so I think w
just stop talking," and, a super crushing blow to my
I got the infamous "Okay," in response.

We played the dance of not talking until a week late
"Hey, let me waste more of your time" text. Afte
it was inevitable. This wasn't going to work. I en
company, and he was a great kisser, but now he j
my Instagram from time to time. Welp, another far

Red Flags
Inconsistent communication.
Went out of town often.

Misfit Tip
If you're confused, there's a reason why. Dating sh

and the most important factors are time and
cation, on the phone or in person. If you're talkingto
and they can't give you either, it's not worth it. Say
e, "Don't forget! Great communication keeps us

Dating Rule #7: We only welcome piec
sides from Popeyes.

And Mr. Married.

We followed one another on Instagram and would s
DMs back and forth until I got the "When are we
out?" message. We met at a brewery in the area, a
beautiful, though a little out of my way. I wasn't su
driving to my own grave or into the arms of my new
husband, but I was down to find out. Words of Adv
you're dating, make sure you let friends and famil
had four people following me on the app.

We met up, and he seemed excited to see me, which
especially since I was dressed like I was going to
Lavigne concert circa 2002. The conversation brim
details about our favorite colors and early childhoo
until he told me he was married. Like, married, mar
"you may kiss your bride" married. He downplaye
was only for the legality, but my vagina dried up,
ready to go.

We talked about surface-level topics the rest of th
and acted like this was an unadulterated meetup. A
of the night, he walked me to my car and had the a
ask me why I didn't kiss on the first date. I will neve
dish, side piece, or sidekick.

Red Flag
Happily Never After?

Misfit Tip
Know your worth and fuck the drama. You can't co
others live their lives, but it's your responsibility

ice you know. You never want to be a liability in
s marriage, better yet your own relationship. Never
·l. No one likes that girl.

Dating Rule #8: If you ask what he do⟨ job and he replies, "I have many jobs,⟩ unemployed.

Mr. Chemistry.

Mr. Chemistry played many roles. Even to this da⟨ know what he did for a career. He was cute in an ar⟨ He had tattoos, wore rings, and took pictures with ⟨ not my type, but I was willing to try something ne⟨

We talked often, but he never made a move or gav⟨ answers. I'd ask him, "What are you looking ⟨ relationship?" or, "When would you like to meet?" ⟨ was always some broad response about "vibes." ⟨ mention us getting together, and the one time we m⟨ he later canceled to hang out with his cousins. Ye⟨ me.

A couple of days later, he suggested we go out ⟨ or a walk. I was open to the idea, but I also knew ⟨ someone cancels on the date, there should be som⟨ an apology or makeup, but it never happened.

Eventually, he caught on to my lack of enthusiasm, ⟨ I made a mention of getting dinner, he said, "Not e⟨ has to be so formal. We don't have to go to di⟨ seemed to continuously dodge the idea of any ⟨ formality when it came to courting someone, and⟨ turn-off. We hadn't been on a date yet, and you'⟨ asking me to settle? Check, please! After a coupl⟨ later, I told him I was giving up on dating, and he un⟨ He was a nice guy, but I'm past settling for anythi⟨

s

em to take anything seriously.

terious.

f.

כ

oks different for everyone. The goal is not to fix,
change a person but find someone who aligns with
yle you want. If making a reservation or taking
lot for your date, just know you'll play that role in
ionship. People will show you who they are fairly
ou just have to see if it's good enough for you.

Dating Rule #9: If you use me as a thera[going to need your copay.

The Cry Baby.

Our first date was a brunch. I was not super exc[seeing him in person just because his energy was a and he looked miserable from the cold when we n the winter. "Sorry, I don't like the cold." But the (well, and he did seem to show more of his person: we warmed up.

After the date, I wanted to see the street art, and w to drive around and look at different types of gr: car drive lasted for about an hour, and I was ready t felt like I was carrying the conversation, and my ir came quickly. Once I was ready to leave, he sugges to a bar and hang out longer.

We did, and the date continued unproblematically.

His personality was regular degular, so to say, b all, he was a stand-up guy. He would complain f to time about the mundane, but little did I know a personality trait. The more we dated, the more how emotionally unstable he was. Our daily conv consisted of reminding him of the positive things and going through how shitty his day was.

After a couple of months, I was exhausted. I could carry the weight of an emotional man and his f: woes on top of my own, and inevitably, I had to le go. I called him on FaceTime and read what I like "Miranda Rights" after being fed up with all his

rating, "This is not good enough for me."
first time I said it out loud. After about 20 minutes, I
conversation and had no intention of ever speaking
again. I got an apology text the next morning, and
atches my Instagram stories from time to time.

rug.

ne was great, but the interview and orientation
e wasn't up for the job.

s
drinking.
ed often.

ted.

p
enough to maintain that level of positivity for
better yet, someone else. It's not your job to be
s emotional crutch. If someone takes from your
e sure they also replenish it. Your light shines, and
cognize it. Make sure they're not taking more than
give; this ain't an all-you-can-eat buffet, honey!

Dating Rule #10: If he emphasizes the being catfished, he is, in fact, the cat

False Advertisement.

False Advertisement was handsome but looked di every picture and didn't have any full-body shots. I met, he mentioned we should FaceTime so he cou I wasn't a catfish.

Disclaimer: If he looks different in every picture, ugly friend of the group.

We FaceTimed, and the conversation was dry, but I might be due to nerves. He was enthusiastic about so I anticipated a better feel once in person. He pl us to go to this street art gallery in the city.

The night of the date, I got a text right before I wa that he was running behind, and I waited around fo I wanted to cancel, but my hair was already done, a fancy lip on. I ended up being late due to traffi understood, which was nice. I called him when I p started walking up to the gallery.

"Where are you? I can't find you." He replied, " I can see you!" I looked across the street to find stopping, home-grown, best-in-show catfish. It wa time in my dating life I went fishing and caught feeder! He was tiny and looked so different in pers everything in me not to turn around and run to my

After the gallery, we went to dinner, and I or appetizer. I tried to make the best of the situatic

asn't going to stay long and had zero appetite. The
ion went from politics to past relationships. He
 story about how he lied to an ex-girlfriend about
)ut of fear of her leaving. You can't make this shit
hed my spring rolls and was ready to roll. We left
ırant, and I booked it into my car. I got home to
ling me how much he appreciated my time. The
as not mutual.

er: I don't do well with awkward situations. So, I
ıy mature adult in this situation, and I text the truth
•n the phone. The next morning, I told him I wasn't
.. The chemistry wasn't there and I'm more of a
ı kind of girl anyways.

s
y, big truck.

p
)uild attraction, but it has to come from something.
 subjective, and if you think he's ugly, he ugly. Das
 nothing wrong with walking away from an ugly ass
cker, especially if he's consumed with making sure
. unrealistic beauty standards.

Dating Rule #11: If he drinks an entire b whiskey on a random Thursday after din know him by name at ABC Liquo

The Gun-Wielding Bacon-Stealer.

Our first date started with him picking me up in a BMW and a long drive to a tapas bar across town. F my door and was very gentlemanly.

At dinner, the menu included a great range of fo personal favorite of bacon-covered dates. I order and our food came quickly. Once the food came o steak, Brussel sprouts, and an assortment of pasta. know each other through quirky banter, and it was r until the infamous bacon-covered dates hit the tab will be the first to admit, I can be a little critical fro time, but I am a firm believer that the small things show a lot of their characteristics in real life.

So, the dates.

I offered a taste, and he winced before even knowir was. It took me back to my marriage when my ex would refuse to try new food. Trust me, all those fur dogs and macaroni and cheese dishes stayed with after that damn marriage, and I was not a fan of pic It's like having a kid. But I digress.

I had one, and we continued talking about our mutua and what we wanted out of a potential new rel Then mid-sentence, I watched as he slowly pick ate all the bacon off the rest of the dates. I was nov an order of soggy bacon-greased dates. That bac

iled and kept talking like nothing happened.
went to dinner, we went back to his place for some
o, sex was not going to happen and, before you
now I shouldn't have gone. But I had my trackers
I was pretty sober, and the energy seemed right, so
th it.

e got to his apartment, it was decorated as I
 bachelorish with different colored changing LED
und the room and a picture of Bob Marley in the
mediately after we got through the door, he placed
 the table right next to the door. I paused and had
t of, "What the fuck is going on here?" He asked
ncomfortable and mentioned he had his concealed
felt okay with it and kept it moving.

n the couch and continued the conversation. I
e was a drinker, as if the three whiskeys he had
r weren't the kicker. He also downed almost half
f another whiskey once we got to his place. We
d after the liquor kicked in, he began to sing every
ong that played on his playlist. Now you might say,
retty normal Nik. We all like to sing songs," but the
e was, he *meant* it. Like he was alone, and no one
r. After his final serenade, my ears and ass were
o home.

d me to my car, and we kissed goodbye.

g the date, communication became inconsistent,
he potential of a second date go down the drain. He
eck in from time to time and began asking to hang
est policy has been honesty, so I mentioned that
ing other men, and with that, he needed to take a
ronically, in the most hetero normative perspective,
at as me being unattainable, and tried harder for us
A month later, we went on a second date.

Once I got to his apartment, the vibe was im different. I had to look for parking, whereas he h reserved for me on the first date. I brushed it off it moving. He ended up surprising me with an e karaoke. We had a good time and eventually wer his place. I got into the car, he placed his hidde my lap and made a joke after I told him I didn't Look, if you like guns, if you don't like guns, I do fuck. I don't want that shit near me. So, if you hadn guessed, that was a red flag, and yes, my dumbass to his home.

Bob Marley and turquoise lighting greeted me upo and it was a lot of the same thing, but this time almost half the bottle of whiskey, causing him to more aggressive when trying to kiss me and asking attention. We played Uno, and he graced me wit concert of his personal favorites. I tried to leave e after he begged, I stayed. I waited until about 3 started to get up to leave, when the dreaded dru came from his mouth, "You aren't going anywhere

He stood in front of me when I tried to get up, a a moment where I searched around the room to I could use as a weapon. I got up with more inte luckily, he got out of the way. I waited at the doo grabbed his gun as he walked me out to my car. were in the hallway, he heard a noise and pointed t if he would use it. Visually uncomfortable, I thou; alibi, and he drunkenly laughed it off as if it wa: deal. This was the last time this situation was ever happen.

The next morning, I told him he made me feel uncon and he apologized but made a mention of not reme

Red Flags
Didn't eat vegetables.

Does This Divorce Make Me Look Fat?

nny jeans.
. with strangers.
eath

p
ates can be more telling than the first. Watch
ctions once they think you're interested. If someone
y oversteps your boundaries and mocks the things
: you uncomfortable, they don't care about how it
u feel. Dating red flags are your "get out of jail"
with no strings attached, and if ignored, you could
 more dangerous and uncomfortable situations.

Dating Rule #12: Sporadic dates will lea with a mouthful of guacamole, but in a go

The One Stop Shop.

I'm usually a "he's a serial killer, be cautious" person, but One Stop Shop's banter was quirky a so I had no issues giving him my number. We talk phone that night, and it was comfortable and ea like talking to a brother or someone I'd known After our first conversation, we decided to meet the week for dinner.

We got Mexican food in the city, and he was late got there, I immediately ordered tacos and guac bitch was starving.

My mindset was, "Someone's going to eat for th us, and I will volunteer as tribute!" I'm talking bea chicken, all inhaled. At one point, he asked me if I because I dropped so much food on my shirt. For couple of hours, we talked about pop culture and h

After dinner, we walked to my car, and I avoided the kiss by talking about rap music until I made my qu my car, side hugs for the win.

The experience of going out with someone that I d an immediate connection with was an enjoyable Without thinking this was my next husband, I engaged and comfortable expressing myself. It of the first times I didn't have to suck it in, orde and seem interested when I really wanted to l right person will make you feel comfortable, bu

:hat every interaction with a new man will make
natically feel something. Personally, it's a way to
ιy anxious trauma as a physical feeling of love, but
 processing. If I had a nickel for every fake love
: had, I would have at least .30 cents, but it's taught
o date moving forward.

.stry.

p

nistry dates are a fun way to get out and meet new
thout expectations. Wear those stretchy pants, order
ιrita, and talk about all the shit you tend to avoid
ginning. You'll get a better understanding of how
ιle perceive you and just how dynamic potential
ιips can actually be.

Dating Rule #13: "It's okay to be a re degular ass bitch."

Mr. He Got Money.

Mr. He Got Money had his shit together. I could a
that he had multiple jobs and his own goals. Hell, ma
a conversation and a job meant wedding bells for
We talked for a week until he asked me out on a da

"Do you like bowling?" Duh! He set up a date
bowling alley near my apartment. There was a super
moment when he said the neighborhood was "a litt
and, meanwhile, I could've walked there from r
He was already there when I arrived. Once again,
him, and he looked so much different than his pictu
slightly disappointed. He seemed very excited to se
I hid being let down.

Bowling was fun, but he mentioned that he spent
the evening and then asked me to take a picture wi

"Do you like taking pictures?"

I immediately responded, "No."

I definitely looked cute that night, but the awkward
came after I said no left a bad taste in my mouth
affect the rest of the evening, but I couldn't stop
"What did he want this picture for?" Additiona
guilty for him constantly talking about the amount
he spent on our date. I felt inclined and insisted o
the tip.

f the date, it felt like he was a little too materialistic
te, but I tried to give him the benefit of the doubt.
and he walked me to my car. It was a lukewarm
I wanted to be open to another date since I wasn't
 materialism was from nerves or lifestyle. A couple
ter, he asked me to dinner at Ruth Kris, and I told
was a little too fancy for me.

 "If you go here for prom, it's fancy." He laughed
sted another place, but I just chalked it up to how
ry different in lifestyle. If only he knew all my
 ere thrifted, and I haven't spent more than $20
 in months. Eventually, I texted him I was giving
ing, and he seemed to completely understand. I
d the efforts, but personally, smaller gestures can
 appreciated. Sometimes you can court me at the
t.

er: Some might say, "Let that man spend that
 you!" But personally, it made me uncomfortable,
 when he told me how much he was spending.

much about money.

)
 and awkward to talk about money, especially on
te. There is an appreciated formality of courting
 but the effort starts to feel like an obligation
 discussed in a certain way. When going into a
tion, state your boundaries and see how your date
 Sometimes, the resume checks out, and the person
dy, but it will forever be an uphill battle if basic
tals don't align.

Dating Rule #14: When people tell yo they are, believe them, even if they say other good things. Also, don't rush the pr dating. It will force you to settle.

The Sweatshirt.

I met Sweatshirt right before my final straw to departure from Dickland. Some would call him card, but he only reiterated my lessons learned c travels.

The first time we talked on FaceTime, he tall about himself, but we had similar interests and a chuckles along the way. After an hour of listenin off the phone, and I said to myself, "I'm never goi from that guy again." Little did I know he would b low-budget magician to cast a spell in my life.

Our first date, we had good conversation, and it was was more attractive in person. On our second date, s odd happened. He gave me his sweatshirt. It might nice gesture for some people, but I didn't get it.

"I want you to remember me," as if foreshado future. It was the second date, and I now was the a man's sweatshirt whose last name I did not kno strange to me. As time progressed, I noticed how and sure he was about me being in his future. After he invited me to a family dinner and told me it wa deal. It turns out it was 12 of his closest family in a room waiting to meet the new woman in his looking back, it was a lot, but I have to be honest, wanted me, and it felt good.

o good at some points. The sex was great, and the
llowing included nights of all the gross shit you
vies. We were falling for one another. Until the red
ly started to creep in. I knew he wasn't "the one"
tedly I was tired of trying. I didn't want to go on
dates and I wanted this to work. His actions didn't
th his words often, and I wanted to believe him so
t I did.

Friday night, he called me and said he didn't
o this anymore. When asking him what happened,
out everything but the kitchen sink on why we
work, and it hurt. How could this man I wasn't
o make me fall for him then break up with me? I
oozled. He kept telling me he was a self-sabotager
me this would happen again. All the efforts, kind
d advances toward the growing relationship were
a factor, and now the sweatshirt was in the trash.

ter, I got an email. He took full accountability and
d for how everything went. That should've been it,
ted so bad to be the success story of, "I normally
his, but I did, and it worked out."

ack together with no real repercussions. We just
where we left off. He agreed to go to therapy, and
y crept back into what we originally had. The red
still there, but I didn't care. We dated for a couple
s until he admitted to cheating on me. He told me
ut with his friends and ended up eating pussy for
. We broke up immediately, and he had the nerve to
t's it?" and I replied, "That's it."

a, por favor! Avoid The Sweatshirt in any way
You'll end up disappointed and confused as to what
ust happened.

update: I randomly bumped into him at a restaurant

a couple of months after our breakup and physically
He was on a date, and I felt like that was an unclose
I didn't end correctly. A couple of weeks later, I ca
and he ended up coming over. We talked for five ho
every aspect of our relationship; the good, the bad
awkward. We both knew it was a closure conversa
while it wasn't needed, I felt better after he left.

He said to me, "I've never done this before, but I
and I agreed. After we said our goodbyes, a we
lifted, and I finally decided to give dating a rest.

Red Flags
Called himself the asshole of his friends.
Littered.
Materialistic.

Misfit Tip
The process of finding love takes time, and if yo
due to loneliness or fear of being single, you'll en
something you don't want. Don't prioritize the
having someone over the quality of the person.
to admit something is just not good enough, ev
someone promises you the world. Promises are d
versions of potential until they turn into consistent

Chapter Six:
Girl, I'm Pressed.

"On my damn self!"

Where We Are Today.

I'm happy, but not in a fuzzy way.

I've fallen in and out of love with myself these
years.

To say it's been all rainbows and sunshine would be
lie. Life post-divorce has been interesting. Betwe
and sitting with the uncomfortable parts of m
I've learned feelings go further than happy and s
includes curiosity, contentment, and stillness.
My new experiences have given me the tools to
healthy relationship with myself and the people i
I had to move to a new city and lose faulty ex
of reality to see that what I longed for I already
tribe, my family, and the people around me that
great. Divorce shined a light on how much love ar
is around me, a feeling I took for granted at times.
Today, I am grateful and full. Of course, life stil
disappointment and moments of sadness, but after c
great feats, everything else seems just a little easie

*"The high road is bumpy and full of potholes, but e
see that life is not about falling in love with someor
with myself."*

For the Patty's in The Back!

The safest way to be petty.

w I couldn't leave this book without one petty
I used to practice the first conversation I'd have if
nped into my ex-husband or *them* together. I know
iess of me ever seeing this man, better yet, this man
·aby mama are the slimmest since we live states
on the rarest occasion, I wanted to be ready for our
rson conversation.

his: We're at our local Wegmans on a Sunday
, and by "we," I mean my forever partner, lover,
fine-ass Mr. Frias. He's in the produce section
or ingredients for Taco Tuesday, and I walk over to
the organic strawberries when something tells me
o. I am met face-to-face with my ex-husband and
s mother. His face goes pale, and he says nothing.
▼ more extensive elevated, self-loving self, I walk
s cart to say hello. I'm nervous, and my stomach is
oat, but I've practiced this memory for years to be
this moment.

v are you?" His girlfriend looks at me and seems
She didn't have to question who I was because
my face from how plastered I was on his social
fore he and I divorced. She looks uncomfortable.
rs quickly, hoping this moment will pass.

good. How are you?" Immediately, his girlfriend
me and tries to introduce herself, "Hi! My name
I cut her off and say, "I know who you are. Very
nally meet you." And the overcrowded grocery
▼ seems empty.

My ex-husband begins to talk about why they w
grocery store and, after a couple of minutes, my
loving, intelligent, fine-as-fuck, sexy ass husband
and says, "Baby! Did we like this brand of guac?"

Before I can answer, my husband sees the situ
introduces himself to my ex-husband like "Hey!
to meet you!" and continues talking to me as if the
there.

The conversation shortly finishes after I reitera
husband we weren't fans of that brand of guacam
told them I have to go.

"It was nice to see you again." My husband and I v
and after we turn around, he gently grabs my left l
and kisses me on the neck.

Drop the fucking mic.

Taking a moment to acknowledge Patty is healtl
all humans, and these thoughts run through our mi
moments are not required. Shit, I just wrote an er
about being alone and how we don't need to tie ou
a relationship for clarity, but it would just be the
We love a good snapback, so prepare your patty
even if it never happens.

I'm not a petty person. It's not in my nature. Bu
representation of your growth, emotionally, men
physically, topped with a man that looks like the
Chris Evans and Michael B. Jordan. Lawd! I'
pregnant thinking about it.

"Prepare your Patty moments, even if they never h

Yelp: An Honest Review.

you for supporting a slight piece of my story."

ivorce 1-star since you can't leave 0 on Yelp.

as hard and fucking sad. There were times I never
 was possible to be so sad. Like crushing sadness,
th a heavy pour of loneliness, and garnished with
. In February 2016, I was physically, mentally, and
ly in the worst shape of my life. I was lost and
nd felt like my comfort superseded my want to do
But the beautiful thing about grief is one day, you
and it doesn't suck as much anymore. The fear of
y it looks, and the normalcy of it will subside, and
ack to doing regular degular shit with people you

ack, I think we would've ended in divorce, even
ax deduction, for the sheer fact that I fucking lost
 happened slowly, and it was dangerous. Every
w I was accepting a subpar life and, eventually,
 it was the only thing I deserved. The benefit of
as it reminded me how strong I was when I forgot,
erated how much I was supported and loved. Not
 I'd recommend, but it's also not something I
urvive.

ne that when I put anyone over myself, I will be put
tions that will eventually make me unhappy. You
ve with and love yourself before sharing it with
d I was missing that exact piece. I traded the ideal
ove that consisted of consideration, responsibility,
idual growth for convenience. Five years since

signing the papers, my personal growth has come
sometimes I have to remind myself I was once tha

I always say divorce was the best thing that has ha
me, and it was because it pushed me to get out of m
zone and take an active role in what I saw in my li

"I now acknowledge April 27th as just another
that's okay."

Acknowledgments

, for always being by my side. To Mom and Dad,
s doing the best you can together. To Cassidy, for
 A1 from Day 1. To Alex, for reminding me to
e gift egg. To Ms. Christine, for always being so
e. To Teeny, for always being my rock. To B town,
s calling. To Hina, for reminding me who I was. To
e, Hiram, and Jenn, for checking in. To Ashia and
or covering the desk when I wanted to cry alone.
, for checking in. To Cheryl, for being there when
ing the lowest. To Nancy, for the reminder of how
gs will eventually be. To Keith, for listening and
 me "believe in you like we do." To Kellyn, for
 to me how much better I deserved. To Jenna, for
ence. To Anthony, for encouraging me to finish
 book. To Janice, for your endless support and
 To Ellen (aka Ma), for teaching me the idea of a
 marriage and having hope that he's out there. To
r the distraction, and to Starbucks, for being the
 small daily pleasure on days when I had nothing
k forward to.

.

About the Author

as is a writer and comedian on a mission to remind
ow dope they are. She is the creator of Girltellme.
blishing platform dedicated to the empowerment of
vriters through comedy, and has articles published
Daily Beast and Forbes. To follow her journey and
igs of other badass women towards writer world
domination head over to Girltellme.com.

Instagram: @girltellme_dotcom

MW00534270